The Mini Rough Guide to
PUGLIA

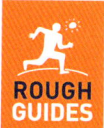

YOUR TAILOR-MADE TRIP
STARTS HERE

Tailor-made trips and unique adventures crafted by local experts

HOW ROUGHGUIDES.COM/TRIPS WORKS

STEP 1

Pick your dream destination, tell us what you want and submit an enquiry.

STEP 2

Fill in a short form to tell your local expert about your dream trip and preferences.

STEP 3

Our local expert will craft your tailor-made itinerary. You'll be able to tweak and refine it until you're completely satisfied.

STEP 4

Book online with ease, pack your bags and enjoy the trip! Our local expert will be on hand 24/7 while you're on the road.

PLAN AND BOOK YOUR TRIP AT
ROUGHGUIDES.COM/TRIPS

How to download your Free eBook

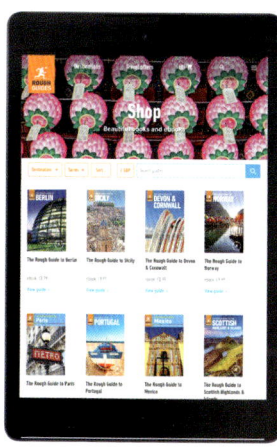

1. Visit **www.roughguides.com/free-ebook** or scan the **QR code** opposite

2. Enter the code **puglia900**

3. Follow the simple step-by-step instructions

For troubleshooting contact: mail@roughguides.com

Contents

- **6** **Introduction**
  - 12 10 Things not to miss
  - 14 A perfect tour of Puglia
  - 16 Beach-hopping in Otranto
  - 18 Salento for foodies
- **20** **History**
- **33** **Places**
  - 33 The Gargano Peninsula
  - 43 Puglia Imperiale
  - 53 Bari and beyond
  - 59 Valle d'Itria
  - 68 The Salento
  - 88 An excursion to Matera
- **95** **Things to do**
  - 95 Culture
  - 96 Nightlife
  - 97 Outdoor activities
  - 102 Shopping
  - 105 Children
  - 106 Festivals and events
- **108** **Food and drink**
- **127** **Travel essentials**
- **142** **Index**

Introduction

Twenty years ago, few foreign tourists took any interest in the heel of Italy's boot and many had never heard of Puglia. Northern Italians tended to regard the region, along with most of the Mezzogiorno (southern Italy) as a land somewhat apart from the rest of Italy, lacking the cultural riches of the north. But from a backward and neglected region Puglia has become the rising star of the south. Most of its tourists are Italian, but an increasing number of foreign Italophiles have been discovering the delights of this southern tip of Italy: from Foresta Umbra and the sands of Gargano to the white-washed hilltop towns of the Valle d'Itria to the Baroque splendour of Lecce. The region is a vast natural larder, the plains and hillsides yielding huge quantities of wine, olive oil and durum wheat, the coasts producing superb fish and seafood. Eating out, whether in a

WHAT'S NEW

With more and more tourists visiting every year (but also thanks to EU funds), Puglia is currently on a path to self-discovery. In 2023, the town of Mattinata, near Foggia, inaugurated its brand-new **Museo Archeologico 'Matteo Sansone'** (see page 36) hosting approximately 2,500 artefacts from the ancient Daunian population donated by the Sansone family to the city. Around the same time, the **museum in Egnazia** (see page 59) presented its new exhibition spaces dedicated to the sea, housed in the museum's spacious cellars. And in 2024, the Italian Navy announced the imminent launch of a **new museum in Bari**, which will be dedicated to lighthouses and coastal towers. But what's constantly evolving is the local cultural offer, with **new food and music festivals** popping up throughout the entire region. There's also a general optimism for the future. After decades of student emigration to northern Italian universities, Puglia is now trying to improve not only its academic offer, but also create more palatable **university towns** – and that benefits tourism, too.

small seaside taverna or at a street stall, is one of the great pleasures of this region.

The land of the two seas

Known as the 'land of the two seas', Puglia has the longest coastline of any region in Italy. Lapped by the Ionian Sea to the west and the Adriatic to the east, it stretches southwards from the 'spur' of the Gargano Peninsula to the tip of the heel of the Italian boot. Most of the region is flat and fertile, with the large plain or 'Tavoliere' of wheat fields around Foggia and further south great swathes of vineyards and silvery-green olive groves. The notable exception to the flat terrain is the spectacular and mountainous Gargano Peninsula where dramatic limestone cliffs plunge into limpid blue waters. The interior of the peninsula is thickly wooded and attracts hikers and bikers, while the pale golden sands are a magnet for beach-lovers. Offshore lie the Isole Tremiti, a small archipelago of tiny islands surrounded by sparkling seas.

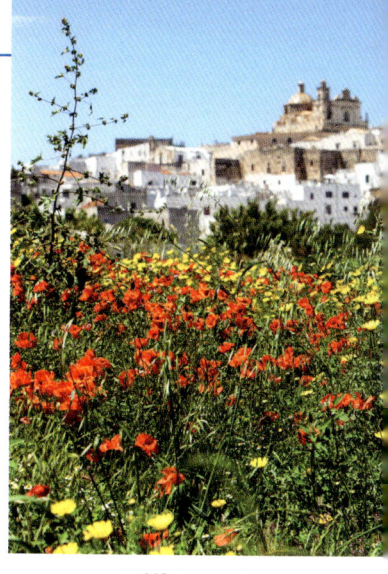

Wildflowers outside the hilltop town of Ostuni

Although it requires a fertile imagination to envisage the famous Roman battles on the plains of Puglia, there are plenty of reminders of the region's long and complex history. Temple ruins and treasures in Taranto's museum are reminders of the golden Greek era; while in Salento some villages have Greek names and roots. From the Roman era there are ruins of amphitheatres, from Norman times castles and

Baia delle Zagare, in the Gargano Peninsula

cathedrals and from Spanish rule a wealth of Baroque.

Truly trulli

On a domestic level the most distinctive and symbolic building of Puglia is the *trullo*, a small, quaint, cone-shaped structure whose origins may go back as far as the Middle Ages. These hobbit-like dwellings crop up in the countryside in the Itria Valley and en masse in Alborebello – designated a UNESCO World Heritage Site, the town boasts over one thousand *trulli*. The region of the Valle d'Itria is also home to the so-called *citta bianche*, or white towns, which crown the hilltops, their dominant cathedrals rising in the distance. Once you arrive in their historic centres (having braved the sprawling outskirts and the challenge of finding a parking space) it is less about specific sights than strolling through a maze of whitewashed alleys, discovering intimate *osterias* or enticing little *salumerias* selling culinary delights.

Almost as iconic as *trulli* are the ancient *masserie*, originally farms that were fortified to ward off invading Turks. Many of these have been stylishly converted to hotels and are very much part of the rapid rise in Puglia's tourism. Often in remote – or seemingly remote – locations, set amid vineyards, olive groves or woodland, they range from simple and affordable *agriturismo*-style farmhouses, where pigs, donkeys and hens graze freely in the grounds, to sophisticated five-star hotels with suites in villas, several swimming pools, a beach club and spa – along with sky-high prices.

A slow pace

When tourism took off in Puglia the region was proclaimed 'the new Tuscany' and the southern city of Lecce was billed 'the Florence of the south'. Anyone familiar with Tuscany might find the comparisons somewhat far-fetched. The parched and predominantly flat landscape of Puglia is a far cry from Tuscany's green and immaculate hills, and while Lecce boasts a riot of Baroque, you won't find Puglian Gothic or Renaissance churches, chapels or *palazzi*. This southern region moreover has a very slow pace of life and a rural simplicity, unchanged by time. Tuscany is more about culture, in Puglia you can seek it out but you can also feel fine about *il dolce far niente* – the enjoyment of idleness. This could be napping by the pool, dipping a toe in the Adriatic, watching the *passeggiata* (evening stroll), feasting on freshly caught fish or downing a glass or two of Primitivo wine in the local bar.

WHEN TO GO

Climate is a key factor if you're considering visiting Puglia. In summer, the heat can be relentless, the resorts impossibly crowded, and the high-season prices for accommodation, car rentals and airfare inflated. On the plus side, summer visitors are rewarded with countless cultural and musical events in most towns and cities. For those who prefer a quiet stay, late spring and autumn are the ideal time to visit: It's still warm, but with fewer tourists and more peaceful beaches. November to January are the wettest months. If you have no choice but to go in high season do as the locals: enjoy a four-hour siesta, join the *passeggiata* as the towns reawaken and dine late in the company of Pugliesi. After all, this is the Mezzogiorno where the locals are welcoming and the pace of life is delightfully slow.

> **NOTES**
>
> *Apulia* is the old Latin name for the region, still sometimes used by English speakers. Locals and all other Italians call it *Puglia*, the modern Latin name, or sometimes the plural, topographical *Le Puglie*, as in *Il Tavoliere delle Puglie*, the vast plain in the north of the region.

The Roman amphitheatre in St Orontius Square, Lecce

Puglia may have lured celebrities (Justin Timberlake and Jessica Biel celebrated their wedding here, Helen Mirren and Meryl Streep have country houses in Salento), but don't expect the sophistication and picture-postcard perfection of Positano, Capri or Sardinia's Costa Smeralda. Although there are luxury *masserie* and some sublime beaches, there are also stretches of unsightly coastal development and a number of neglected towns or villages. Although you can find glamorous parties on Gallipoli's beaches, nightlife is generally low-key and eateries tend to be small family-run tavernas rather than sophisticated restaurants. Parts of Puglia are quite wild and underdeveloped. It can still feel remote, but in the very best sense of the word.

A foodie heaven

The region has a tradition of *cucina povera* (poor cuisine) which means remarkably flavoursome dishes based on an abundance of fresh,

INTRODUCTION

> ## SUSTAINABLE TRAVEL
>
> Puglia is a great destination for eco-aware travellers, with many **eco-friendly places to stay** (see www.ecobnb.com), protected natural areas and a vegan-sensitive culture.
>
> With a mostly flat terrain, **biking** is a popular way to explore the region. The many tried and tested itineraries range from easy, family-friendly coastal rides through pretty towns and beach areas to more rural excursions through olive groves, *masserie* (traditional country houses), and *trulli*. Expert cyclists might choose the more mountainous bike itineraries around Gargano. But Puglia also has an ancient tradition of **walking trails**, having been the main passageway for pilgrims who wanted to reach Jerusalem throughout the centuries. Lovers of hiking will appreciate the many scenic country roads and *tratturi* (sheep paths). The website www.viaggiareinpuglia.it lists popular walking and biking itineraries, with information about the best stops for food and sightseeing. The **local cuisine** features lots of plant-based dishes, so vegetarians and vegans won't have a hard time finding great food, even in the most remote trattorias. More sophisticated and creative vegan options abound in the cities. To help counter **over-tourism**, avoid the high season and do as the locals do: choose a slow pace of life.

local and seasonal ingredients. The diet is a very simple, healthy one, based on vegetables, fruit, fresh fish, top-quality olive oil and healthy pasta made with durum flour. 'Seasonal', 'slow food' and 'farm-to-table' are not new to the food scene – it's how things have been for centuries. The signature pasta is *orecchiette* (little ears) which you can see being made by hand in the backstreets of old Bari. The classic and hugely popular dish is *orecchiette alle cime di rapa*, translated as *orecchiette* with turnip tops but actually more like a leafy broccoli. With 800km (497 miles) of coastline, it's not surprising that seafood is an essential element of Puglia's cuisine. You can feast on raw sea urchins straight from fishing boats, tuck into bowls of clams or mussels or savour steamed octopus or stuffed cuttlefish.

10 Things not to miss

1. **GARGANO PENINSULA**
   Ravishingly beautiful spur with stunning coastline and an ancient forest for hiking and biking. See page 33.

2. **TREMITI ISLANDS**
   Glorious group of tiny, unspoilt islands, surrounded by glittering turquoise seas. See page 40.

3. **CASTEL DEL MONTE**
   A unique medieval masterpiece reflecting the humanism of its founder, Frederick II of Swabia. See page 44.

4. **TRANI**
   Elegant coastal town with a dramatically sited Romanesque cathedral and a finely restored historic centre and port. See page 49.

5. **ALBEROBELLO**
   The centre of Puglia's famous *trulli* – the quaint, conical-roofed houses. See page 61.

6. **MARTINA FRANCA**
   Large and lively town, known for its finely preserved Baroque monuments and gastronomy. See page 63.

7. **LECCE**
   Puglia's Baroque gem, packed with lavish architecture and fanciful facades. See page 71.

8. **OTRANTO**
   Historic port with a picturesque old quarter, stunning cathedral and good beaches nearby. See page 78.

9. **GALLIPOLI**
   Charming historic town with fishing harbour and good seafood restaurants. See page 83.

10. **MATERA (IN BASILICATA)**
    Fascinating troglodyte town of ancient grottoes and rock-hewn churches. See page 88.

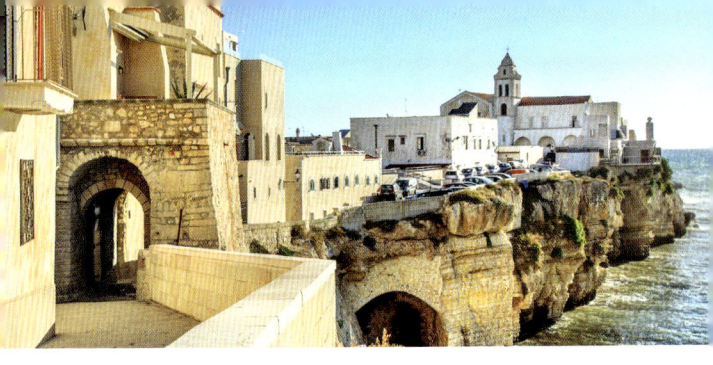

A perfect tour of Puglia

ITINERARY

DAY 1
Vieste. Make the Gargano Peninsula your base for three nights (it's a long haul from Brindisi or Bari airports). Stay at the seaside resort of Vieste, surrounded by coves, cliffs and excellent beaches. Stroll through the historic centre, feast on fish creations at *Il Capriccio* (see page 120) then chill out on one of the golden-sand beaches.

DAY 2
Gargano National Park. Join a cycling or hiking tour to explore the beautiful 15,000-acre Foresta Umbra.

DAY 3
Tremiti Islands. Take a ferry from Vieste to the glorious Tremiti Islands (note that there are no ferries from Vieste during off season). These bite-sized isles are still largely unspoilt despite many summer visitors. Renowned for dazzling blue-green waters and a fascinating coastline of sun-bleached cliffs, grottoes and rocky coves, they are perfect for diving, swimming and boat trips. Explore historic sights at San Nicola, then take a boat to the pine-clad San Domino.

DAY 4
Trani. Drive south along the coast to Trani, a beautiful port and fishing village with a prosperous air. The showpiece is the dazzling white cathedral, set dramatically against the deep blue sea. Discover the historic quarter and colourful port with bars and restaurants.

DAY 5
Valle d'Itria. Discover the white towns and the *trulli* of the Itria Valley. Head south to Alberobello, capital of *trulli*, with around 1,500 of the quaint conical-roofed dwellings. Less touristy are the lovely hilltop towns of Locorotondo or Ostuni to the east. Spend an evening in the beautiful Baroque town of Martina Franca south of Alberobello. Join the *passeggiata*, dine in the historic centre and check out the evening cultural programme in this lively university town.

DAYS 6 AND 7
Lecce. Head south to Lecce and stay a couple of days. This is the Baroque jewel of Puglia so spend time strolling the squares and streets of the old town, absorbing the exuberant facades of churches and *palazzi*. Combine culture with a spot of retail therapy by checking out the *cartapesta* (papier-mâché) workshops and the chic shops selling olive oil and local pasta, then dine on traditional *cucina povera* (food for the poor) at *Alle Due Corti* (see page 124).

DAY 8
Otranto. Drive south to the lovely port of Otranto, ending your tour on the Adriatic coast. Visit the unique Romanesque cathedral with a remarkable floor mosaic, enjoy seafood specialities at *LaltroBaffo* (see page 125) and spend the rest of the day relaxing on one of the fine sandy beaches.

Beach–hopping in Otranto

9AM

Crystalline waters. Start your beach-hopping day at the beach of Torre dell'Orso. The 800m-long bay is known for its white sands bordered on two sides by pine forests, which protect it even on the windiest days. Get a cappuccino at the beach bar then go for an early morning swim in the beautiful crystal-clear waters.

10.30AM

Sea arches and caves. Driving south for about 4km, you'll get to Torre Sant'Andrea. The beach here is small, but the real attraction is the Faraglioni, one of Salento's most picturesque views. These white rocky formations, featuring caves and sea arches, create a stunning contrast against the turquoise waters they are immersed in, making for the perfect photo opportunity. To reach them from the Caletta, walk northwards along the cliffs.

11.30AM

Pine trees and Turkish invasions. Drive towards Otranto for about 10min and you'll get to Baia dei Turchi. The beach, currently a nature reserve, can be reached with a 10min walk through the pine forest or by shuttle for a small fee. Baia dei Turchi also has historic significance: it's where the Ottomans landed when they invaded Puglia. To cool off after the long walk, jump in the water for a short snorkelling session.

12.30PM

Hungry? Drive for about 15min to Otranto and have a light lunch at *La Locanda del Porto* (Via del Porto; www.lalocandadelporto.it), a lovely fish restaurant. It's good to stay away from the sun during the hottest hours, so once you're done take a walk along the harbour. Don't forget to drink an espresso before getting back on the road.

3PM

Family beach and a Neolithic site. A 20min drive will take you to Porto Badisco, a coastal area surrounded by gorgeous cliffs, offering a combination of rocky stretches and sandy beaches. The water is shallow and calm, making it perfect for children. An important attraction here is the Grotta dei Cervi, a cave featuring Neolithic paintings of deer. The cave is closed to the public for conservation reasons, but you can book a tour of the area to learn more about the caves (www.guide.puglia.it).

5PM

The Maldives of Salento. After a refreshing swim in Porto Badisco, get back in the car for a 30min drive to Pescoluse, also known as the Maldives of Salento. Featuring fine, white sand and perfectly clear water, this beach is reminiscent of the tropical islands it's named after. After this long and eventful day, it's time to relax. Order an aperitivo at one of the beach bars, and just enjoy the view while waiting for the sunset.

Salento for foodies

9AM

But first, coffee. Start the day at *Caffè Alvino* in Lecce (Piazza Sant'Oronzo 30), overlooking the gorgeous piazza, and enjoy a *caffè salentino ghiacciato*, a local interpretation of iced coffee made with almond milk and lots of ice cubes.

9.30AM

Sweet dreams. For the best pastries in town, head to *Pasticceria Natale* (Via Salvatore Trinchese 7) just a block away, and stock up on *pasticciotti*. This bakery is known for its *fruttone* filling, made with almond cream and quince. For a true taste of Italy, you might also want to try their Sicilian *cassata*.

10AM

Olive oil straight from the makers. It's time to head to the coast, but first make a stop at Oleificio Ciccarese (Via Est Nardó Loc. Li Tumi; www.oleificiociccarese.it), an olive press near Copertino. See how oil is made and taste the press's best oil varieties. Their small bottles make for great gifts.

11AM

To market, to market. Drive to Porto Cesareo, Salento's fish capital. On Thursdays, visit the food market — it's an explosion of colours and smells, with a huge variety of fish straight from the fishermen's boats. On any other day, walk along Via Silvio Pellico, known as 'the street of fishmongers'. Red shrimps are the speciality here, both raw or cooked, together with sea urchins and mussels.

1PM

Fried mix. Eat at *L'Angolo del Gusto* (Via Silvio Pellico 25; https://langolo-del-gusto.metro.biz), a friendly restaurant serving delicious fried seafood and a variety of traditional and creative dishes, alongside the staples of Apulian cuisine such as *orecchiette alle cime di rapa*.

2.30PM

Cheers! Head south towards Gallipoli, but first stop at Cantina Coppola 1489 (www.cantinacoppola.it), a historic, family-run winery that offers tours and tastings (*degustazioni*). Event hours vary, so it's advisable to call ahead.

6.30PM

Aperitivo at sunset. Watch the sun set with a glass of wine at *Mivida* in Gallipoli (Riviera Nazario Sauro 6). To tickle your hunger before dinner, order a cheese platter which includes delicious local mozzarella, or a fish tartare.

8.30PM

Dulcis in fundo. End the day with a lively meal at *I Portici* (Corso Roma 13; www.iporticigallipoli.it), a loud and simple eatery specializing in Apulian pizzas and *pinsa* (a lighter version), accompanied by local craft beers. Then enjoy a *passeggiata* with gelato along the chic Lungomare of Gallipoli.

History

Between the East and the West, with long and exposed coastlines on either side, Puglia has always been vulnerable to attack and invasion. Ever since the arrival of seafarers from across the Adriatic Sea, foreign powers have fought for a stake here and made their lasting mark. The Greeks and Romans, Lombards and Normans, Angevins and Aragonese, Habsburgs and Bourbons have all vied for control here at one time or another, leaving behind a beguiling cultural hybrid.

A replica of the ancient Neanderthal, the Altamura Man, discovered in Lamalunga Cave

Magna Graecia

It was during the Bronze Age, from around 1700 BC, that the Greeks first established links with southern Italy, the Mycenaeans from mainland Greece and the Minoans from Crete, forming trading links. But it was another four centuries or so before Greek settlers founded colonies in southern Italy. Exiles from Sparta founded Taras (modern Taranto), which became the most prosperous town in Magna Graecia in the third century BC and a focus of Greek culture. Other Greek city states were founded at Hydrus (Otranto) and Kallipolis (Gallipoli). Little remains of this golden era although a pair of columns from Taranto's Doric Temple survive and there is a veritable treasure trove of finds from ancient Tara in the city's Archeological Museum.

Roman rule

By the time the Romans were advancing from the north, Magna Graecia had been weakened by wars between the city states and invasions

NOTES

The oldest human remains discovered in Puglia are those of the calcified Altamura Man, discovered in a karst sinkhole in the Grotta di Lamalunga near Altamura. Recent tests show that the fossil (which is still in the cave) is that of a Neanderthal man, who died between 128,000 and 187,000 years ago.

by Etruscans. The Romans rapidly expanded throughout the region. Taras (Taranto) rebelled against the Romans and sought the military assistance of Pyrrhus, King of Epirus in north-western Greece. After early failures at the hands of the King, Rome defeated the Tarentines and occupied Taranto in 272 BC. They rapidly colonized and Latinized the region and by 266 BC, when the Romans took Brundisium (modern Brindisi), the whole of southern Italy had come under their control.

During the Second Punic War Hannibal invaded Italy (218 BC), crossing the Alps and establishing a hold over the north of Italy. Reinforced by Gallic tribesmen he marched south, and in 216 BC annihilated a huge Roman army at the celebrated Battle of Cannae. Carthaginian forces remained in Puglia whilst Hannibal attempted to forge sufficient Italian alliances to make good a permanent occupation of Italy. He failed in the enterprise and was forced to retreat to Africa where Rome defeated Carthage at Zama in 202 BC, bringing an end to the war.

Rome then ruled the whole of the peninsula for some six centuries. Puglia was unified and acquired great importance with all

Remains of the Doric Temple (Temple of Poseidon) in Taranto, dating back to the sixth century BC

the trade routes to eastern Mediterranean countries converging on the region through the port of Brindisi and along the Appian and Trajan ways. Today Roman remains are dotted across Puglia, including the columns terminating the Appian Way at Brindisi and the large amphitheatre and Roman theatre at Lecce.

The dark ages

Following the fall of the Roman Empire in the west in AD 476, there was a long, dark age for Italy with successive invasions by barbarians. In 535 the forces of the eastern Emperor Justinian under the command of Belisarius fought a succession of campaigns against the Goths. In 536 Belisarius crossed to the mainland. Most of southern Italy welcomed the Byzantine army, but the reconquest was curtailed by Lombard invaders who descended from the north and confined the Byzantines to the extreme south.

The next wave of invaders were the Saracens from North Africa, including Arabs, Spanish Muslims and Berbers. Short-lived emirates were established at Bari and Taranto.

The eastern Empire continued to rule parts of the mainland south and in 975 began a successful military campaign of further re-conquest. Effective Byzantine imperial rule was established over the whole of Puglia, as well as Calabria and Basilicata. This resulted in tremendous waves of Greek settlers who were arriving from the east so that by the end of the tenth and early eleventh centuries Puglia was, to a large extent, culturally Greek. This Greek influence is still strongly felt in eleven municipalities of Salento, whose inhabitants still speak Griko, a neo-Greek dialect that was recently granted the 'endangered language' status by the European Union.

King Pyrrhus invaded Apulia in the third century BC

Norman invasion and conquest

The earliest Normans to come to Puglia were knights on pilgrimage to Christian shrines, most notably to St Michael at Monte Sant'Angelo in the Gargano. This gradually gave rise to Papal encouragement of a Norman military invasion by the Hauteville dynasty from northern France, to drive out the Byzantines. This Papal-Norman alliance led to the annexation of Sicily and large parts of southern Italy including Puglia. The celebrated Crusader Robert de Hauteville (1015–85), who was nicknamed 'Guiscard' or 'the Crafty', ousted Lombards, Saracens and Byzantines and became Duke of Apulia, Calabria and Sicily. In 1130 Roger II of the Hauteville dynasty was crowned the first king of Sicily. His holdings included most of southern Italy. Puglia benefited from the peace and security of the times. Norman rule also left an indelible stamp on Puglia with the construction of both castles and monuments, and magnificent cathedrals, too. Puglia's port cities transformed into harbours for the Crusades and enjoyed a flourishing trade with the Levant.

Seventeenth-century map of Gallipoli

Stupor Mundi

In the late twelfth century the Norman dynasty was replaced by the German House of Hohenstaufen, bringing Sicily and southern Italy within the sway of the Holy Roman Emperor. The Hohenstaufen Holy Roman Emperor Henry VI was succeeded by his son Frederick II when he died in 1197. Known as *Stupor Mundi* or 'Wonder of the World', Frederick (1194–1250) was one of the most significant rulers of the Middle Ages. At European level he claimed pre-eminence over all other secular rulers and struggled to wrest from the papacy its burgeoning political power and return it to its true Christian ethos of, as he saw it, purity and saintliness. He introduced a unified legal system, promoted the arts and sciences and encouraged a blend of Islamic, Jewish and Christian cultures. He left his mark with 29 castles in Puglia, including his enduring monument, the Castel del Monte.

> **NOTES**
>
> In 1480 a Turkish fleet with some eighteen thousand soldiers laid siege to Otranto, slaughtering the majority of males over 15. Around eight hundred of the survivors were offered mercy if they renounced the Christian faith. They refused and were beheaded. Their skulls and relics are preserved in the Chapel of Martyrs in Otranto's Cathedral.

French and Spanish

The death of Frederick II in 1250 marked the end of the Hohenstaufen dynasty and the beginning of a long period of decline for Puglia, which took place under various foreign rulers. The Hohenstaufen rulers were succeeded by the Angevins, from central France, followed by the Spanish House of Aragon. In Puglia the economy declined drastically, the population decreased and many towns and villages were abandoned. Under the Spaniards (1503–1707) trade suffered from heavy taxes, corruption was rife among Spanish officials and landowners exploited the common people.

The death in 1700 of the childless Charles II of Spain, who was the last of the Spanish Habsburgs, prompted the War of the Spanish Succession (1700–15). Under the Treaty of Utrecht in 1713 southern Italy was ceded to the Austrian Habsburgs. The arrangement only lasted until 1738 when the Bourbon King Charles VII expelled the Austrians and established the Kingdom of the Two Sicilies as an independent kingdom under the Bourbon dynasty.

In the early nineteenth century Puglia, like most of the rest of Italy, was controlled by Napoleonic France. Although French occupation lasted only nine years (1805–14), it was a period of

Taranto in 1834

economic and agricultural reform not previously seen even in post-medieval times. After the fall of Napoleon the Kingdom of the Two Sicilies reverted to the Bourbons after the Congress of Vienna. By its last decade Bourbon rule was despised for its oppression. The continued unrest set the stage for Garibaldi, leader of the Risorgimento and the campaign for Unification.

From Unification to the present

With his so-called 'Thousand' (volunteers) Garibaldi sailed into Sicily in 1860 and from there into southern Italy, heralding the flight of the last Bourbon, Francis II, from Naples. In 1861 Vittorio Emanuele II was proclaimed king and the region became part of the Kingdom of Italy. But southern Italians were soon disillusioned with life as part of a new unified Italy. Taxes rose, the economy declined and only one percent of the population was eligible to vote. There were abortive uprisings, some savagely repressed. The only escape from poverty seemed to be emigration and in the last decades of the nineteenth century enormous numbers of southern Italians sought a new life overseas, mainly in North or South America.

It was not until after World War I that Puglia saw any stability or prosperity. The malaria crisis which had ravaged Italy, particularly the south, was finally brought under control, though was not completely eradicated until the 1960s. Poor farming conditions and domestic discomfort, brought about by the parched terrain, was greatly alleviated by the Great Aqueduct in 1939 (see page 81) and then by modern wells cut deep into the rocks.

During the 1950s and '60s, unemployment led to another mass migration, with southerners leaving to find jobs in northern Italy, which was enjoying an economic boom, and also to other parts of Europe. The trend declined as economic conditions improved in the south. Today Puglia is a far more productive area, both agriculturally and industrially. Thanks to its huge production of wheat and pasta it became known as the breadbasket of Italy. It produces 40 percent of the country's olive oil and is one of Italy's largest wine-making regions. Small food-processing industries are widespread, but the main industrial centres are Bari and Taranto. Albeit on a smaller scale than before, migration is still an issue with young Pugliesi (and southern Italians in general), particularly the well-educated. Youth-unemployment is high and many ambitious young Italians are discouraged by the scarcity of jobs, particularly the most rewarding ones, not to mention *clientelismo* – political patronage and nepotism. Meanwhile waves of migrants have been arriving on southern Italian shores, including Puglia, despite the fact that migrant rescue ships are currently banned from docking in Italy.

Alberobello in 1899

In the first decade of the twenty-first century, low-cost carriers opened up the region to British tourists and the meteoric rise in visitor numbers had a highly beneficial effect on Puglia's economy. The region has since seen the rejuvenation of towns and historic centres, the restoration of many museums and the transformation of manor farms (*masserie*) into luxury accommodation.

But in 2020 and 2021 the Covid-19 pandemic broke out, and Puglia suffered much like the rest of Italy

Olive oil is big business

with a dramatic decline in visitor numbers. Thanks to the recovery funds granted to Italy by the European Union, Puglia managed to emerge from the crisis stronger than ever, and with a new goal in mind: to become a new exclusive, luxury destination not only for Italians but also for international tourists. While this has helped improve the local economy and expand the tourist offer, especially in the Val D'Itria and Brindisi areas, locals now complain about over-tourism, unjustified prices and reduced authenticity. Meanwhile, a 2023 ISTAT (Italian National Institute of Statistics) report defines Puglia as Italy's 'most dynamic region', thanks to its significant growth not only in tourism, but in most industry sectors. Bari is currently the number one city in southern Italy for employment rates – a sign that things for Puglia are really looking upwards.

Chronology

700,000 BC Paleolithic Man inhabits caves such as the Grotta dei Cervi.
Third/second millennium BC Messapians migrate from Dalmatia to Puglia.
Eighth century BC Greek colonists establish Taras (Taranto) and other cities.
275 BC Roman defeat of Greeks at Beneventum, last battle of the Pyrrhic War.
216 BC Hannibal defeats Romans at Cannae.
190 BC Romans extend Via Appia to Brindisi.
AD 476 Fall of western Roman empire. Gothic tribes invade.

Italian Carabinieri

Sixth century Byzantine re-conquest of parts of Italy including Puglia.
Ninth century Saracen invasions from Sicily destroy parts of Puglia.
1130 Norman invader Roger II rules southern Italy.
1220 Holy Roman Emperor Frederick II starts his thirty-year domination of the region.
1266–1282 Angevin rule in southern Italy.
1282–1500 Spain, France and the Papacy vie for control over southern Italy.
1501 King Ferdinand of Spain incorporates southern Italy, including Puglia, into his Habsburg empire.
1713 Treaty of Utrecht: Austria inherits Habsburg lands including southern Italy.
1738 Treaty of Vienna: Puglia passes to the Spanish House of Bourbon.
1860 The unification of Italy process brings the end of Bourbon rule.
1880–1915 Massive exodus from southern Italy to the New World.
1950–60s Mass migration from southern to northern Italy, and Europe.
2018 Italian general election. Hung Parliament leads to a coalition.
2019 Matera (in Basilicata) is named European Capital of Culture. Migrants continue to reach Italy's southern shores.
2020 In March, Bergamo in Lombardy becomes the European epicentre of Covid-19. Italy suffers one of the highest death rates in Europe.
2021 Mario Draghi, former President of the European Central Bank, is invited to form a national unity government. Italy receives its first payment from the EU's €750 billion recovery fund.
2024 Puglia's employment rate increases across sectors and tourism ramps up. The Alta Murgia National Park in Bari is declared a UNESCO Geopark.

Vieste, beautifully set on a tip of the Gargano Peninsula

Places

The 'land of two seas', Puglia stretches 400km (248 miles) from north to south, between the Ionian and Adriatic seas. A car is the best way to get around but you would need at least three weeks to take in all the highlights. The majority of visitors arrive at the capital, Bari, explore the whitewashed hill villages and *trulli* of the Valle d'Itria and then head south to the Salentine Peninsula. Those with more time can take in the alluring but less accessible Gargano promontory in the north of the region. The chapter starts here and moves south along the coast to Bari, through the Valle d'Itria to the Baroque city of Lecce and the coastal towns and beaches of Salento. Last but not least is the city of Matera, the jewel of the region of Basilicata, just across the border from Puglia.

The Gargano Peninsula

Highlights
- **Foresta Umbra**, see page 34
- **Monte Sant'Angelo**, see page 34
- **Vieste**, see page 37
- **Peschici**, see page 38
- **Rodi Garganico**, see page 39
- **Isole Tremiti**, see page 40
- **Il Tavoliere**, see page 42

The only real mountains of Puglia are clustered around the Gargano promontory, a thickly forested peninsula that juts out into the Adriatic to form 'the spur' of the boot of Italy. This is one of Italy's most beautiful regions, discovered but not yet wrecked by tourism. The coastline is truly spectacular, boasting craggy, bleached limestone cliffs, pale sandy beaches, grottoes, rocky coves and beguiling blue-green waters. In contrast is the thickly wooded wild interior, where only dappled sunlight penetrates the trees.

For most foreign tourists the Gargano is still regarded as rather out of the way. The road from sprawling Manfredónia, gateway to the promontory, is very slow-going, whether you opt for the serpentine coastline or the hairpin bends through the mountains. From Bari airport it takes at least 2 hours 30 minutes by car to the main resort of Vieste. In July and August large numbers of northern Italians flock here – and to the lovely little Tremiti Islands offshore. Outside these months it's relatively quiet. By October, when it is normally still warm and the sea water averages 20˚C, many tourist amenities have closed down completely and don't get going again until late spring.

Foresta Umbra

In the heart of the Gargano National Park the **Foresta Umbra** ❶ is an ancient 15,000-acre forest of beech, chestnut, Aleppo pines and oaks. The only true forested area in Puglia, this protected region is the habitat of deer, foxes and hares and is home to most of the varieties of orchids indigenous to Europe. The forest has marked trails and is becoming increasingly popular for guided hiking and cycling tours.

Monte Sant'Angelo

The Gargano's best-known medieval town is **Monte Sant'Angelo** ❷, a remarkable little pilgrimage town, which was designated a UNESCO World Heritage Site in 2011. It perches on a rocky spur at 800m (2,625ft) and affords jaw-dropping views over the Bay of Manfredónia. Whether you're a worshipper or not, it's well worth the journey up tortuous bends to see the old quarter with its picturesque alleys and monuments. Avoid Sundays and on no account go on September 29, St Michael's Day, when thousands of pilgrims flock to the hilltop, some climbing all the way up on

Inside the Santuario di San Michele, Monte Sant'Angelo

foot from Vieste. Their target is the fifth-century **Santuario di San Michele** (www.santuariosanmichele.it; free), located in a grotto where the archangel is said to have appeared three times to the Bishop of Siponto. From the double-arched Gothic portico, flanked by an octagonal belfry, a staircase of 86 steps takes you down to the dimly lit sanctuary. The cave is entered through a pair of beautiful bronze doors, depicting biblical scenes and believed to have been cast in Constantinople. Inside the grotto are a sixteenth-century statue of the Archangel and a twelfth-century marble episcopal throne.

Opposite the Sanctuary steps lead down to the **Tomba di Rotari**. Originally believed to be a Lombard tomb, it is now thought to be a twelfth-century baptistry. Entry is via the remains of the medieval Chiesa di San Pietro, destroyed in a nineteenth-century earthquake. At the uppermost part of the town is the much-modified Norman **castle**, with fine views and one surviving tower, the Torre dei Giganti. In Mattinata, the **Museo Archeologico Nazionale di Mattinata 'Matteo Sansone'** (Via Tasso 1; http://museipuglia.cultura.gov.it; charge), inaugurated in 2022, houses 2,500 artefacts found locally and attributed to the Daunian peoples who inhabited the area in the seventh century BC. The collection includes beautiful pottery, coins, and steles, all donated by the family of Matteo Sansone, a local pharmacist and collector.

From Mattinata to Vieste the inland road climbs up steeply for about 18km (11 miles), and for the next 24km (15 miles) twists downwards through the wild landscape before reaching Vieste. The

Spiaggia di Pizzomunno and its monolith

much slower coastal road, via beaches and tourists resorts, has some fabulous stretches of sands, including the **Baia delle Zagare**, an exquisite crescent of white sand beach, with two large rocks rising from turquoise waters.

Vieste

The largest resort in the region, **Vieste** ❸ is beautifully set on a tip of the Gargano Peninsula, surrounded by caves, cliffs and golden-beaches. Among its attractions are the boat trips, skirting the cave-riddled coast, and excursions across to the Isole Tremiti (Tremiti Islands, see page 40). Tourist development dominates the outskirts of Vieste but the town has a charming historic quarter of whitewashed houses, medieval alleys and arches. The dominant monuments are the Romanesque **cathedral**, remodelled over the centuries, and the **castle** (closed to the public), built by Frederick II at the highest point of the town.

Vieste is famous for its beaches. Two of the best are the spacious **Spiaggia di Pizzomunno**, south of the resort, named after the 20m (66ft)-high rock monolith rising from the sands and the huge **Spiaggia di Scialmarino**, 4.5km (3 miles) to the north. There are also beaches within walking distances. As in most Puglian resorts the larger swathes of sand are blanketed with regimented rows of sun-loungers and parasols but after August everything, including the tourists, seems to disappear.

> **NOTES**
>
> On the rocks between Vieste, Peschici and Rodi Garganico, look out for the dozen or so wooden contraptions suspended over the sea, known as *trabucchi*. Traditionally used for fishing, these consist of a large platform and long wooden poles, beams, ropes and pulleys to lower nets into the water and bring them up with the catch. Some of the *trabucchi* have been restored and three of them have been converted into enticing sea-view restaurants.

Peschici

Peschici

From Vieste the SS89 winds through olive groves, then snakes its way up into the wooded mountains before descending to Peschici. A stop at the roadside stalls selling cheese, olive oil and chillies will make a welcome break from the hairpin bends. Perched high above the sea **Peschici** ❹ is a charming fishing town where white houses tumble down the cliffside. More intimate than Vieste, the seaside resort has a lively little *centro storico*, a hilltop castle and dozens of inviting outlets for local Pugliese products, including the highly regarded local olive oil. You can learn all about it at **Al Vecchio Frantoio** (www.facebook.com/alvecchiofrantoioranieri), which has an old olive press and quality extra-virgin olive oils (lemon-flavoured is a speciality), along with explanations and tastings. From here the cobbled street leads up to **Castello di Peschici** (www.cultura.gov.it/luogo/castello-di-peschici; free), dating back to the tenth century but much remodelled. The ground floor, formerly used as a prison and arms depot, is now a museum with a gruesome collection of torture devices.

Ferries from Peschici depart daily in season for the Isole Tremiti. Another option is a coastal boat trip to see bizarrely shaped and fancifully named grottoes, quiet coves and secluded beaches. Taking a dip in the pristine sea is always an option.

Rodi Garganico

The SS89 continues its scenic switchback route through the mountains, cutting through forests of lush pines, then dropping down to the sprawling, non-descript resort of San Menaio. The beach stretches all the way to **Rodi Garganico** ❺ which, like Vieste and Peschici, is picturesquely set on a headland with houses built up on the spur. It is more down to earth than Vieste or Peschici and a railway divides the sea from the town, but the old centre has plenty of charm. Steep streets, where washing flaps in the breeze, lead up to the historic centre with its quiet cobbled streets and spacious main piazza. The resort has some lovely white beaches but you would be hard-pushed to find space here in July or August.

East of Rodi Garganico lie two coastal, fish-filled lakes, Lesino and Varano, separated from the sea by sand dunes. These are both popular with birdwatchers, who come to see species on the Africa–Europe migratory route.

PADRE PIO

From a medieval farming hamlet, San Giovanni Rotondo, west of Manfredónia, has become a global centre of pilgrimage visited by around seven million visitors a year. Perched on a hill and accessed via a twisting road, the town is inextricably linked with the Capuchin friar, Padre Pio (1887–1968), a stigmatist and miracle-worker who lived and worked here as a healer of the sick for 52 years. Father Pio was proclaimed a saint in 2002 and is worshipped across the region. His remains lie in the crypt of the Convent of Santa Maria delle Grazie, which was enlarged in the late 1950s to accommodate the overflow of pilgrims. By the Millennium space was again at a premium and the leading Italian architect, Renzo Piano, was commissioned to build a new church. It is only 16m (52ft) high but has capacity for 6,500 worshippers, one of the largest in Italy. There are no less than five annual festivals celebrating the life of the saint. His image is ubiquitous, in bars, shops and garages, and the favourite souvenirs are kitsch little Padre Pios.

Isole Tremiti

An archipelago in the Adriatic Sea, 22km (14 miles) north of the Gargano Peninsula, the **Isole Tremiti** ❻ are renowned for their natural beauty and dazzling clear waters. '*Tremiti*' means 'tremors' and derives from the islands' renowned seismic activity. This has also characterized their landscape of jagged white cliffs, sandy coves and sparkling grottoes along the coastline. Only two of the five are inhabited and the population is around two hundred.

The islands have traditionally been a place of exile. Caesar Augustus banished his granddaughter, Julia the Younger, to San Domino for her promiscuity and Charlemagne had his father-in-law, accused of conspiracy, sent here after removing his eyes and limbs. The islands were used as a penal colony in the nineteenth century and in 1938 Mussolini banished hundreds of homosexuals to an internment camp on San Domino.

View of San Nicola

The islands can be reached by ferry service from May to September from Manfredónia, Vieste, Peschici and Rodi Garganico. (The only year-round service to the islands is from Termoli, on the coast of Molise.) There is also an affordable helicopter service (€64 return, 20min journey) to San Domino from Foggia (www.alidaunia.it). Cars are not permitted on the islands. The ferry trip alone is worthwhile, especially from Vieste, where you can enjoy stunning views of the coast with its white cliffs and beaches before the boat heads out to the islands.

San Nicola

The fast *aliscafi* (hydrofoils) from Gargano normally arrive at the rocky little island of **San Nicola**, with its picturesque port and colourful fishing boats beached on the pebble shore. From here you can take a boat trip around the islands and be dropped off at San Domino, returning to San Nicola on one of the hourly ferries. Alternatively, there are water taxis between the islands.

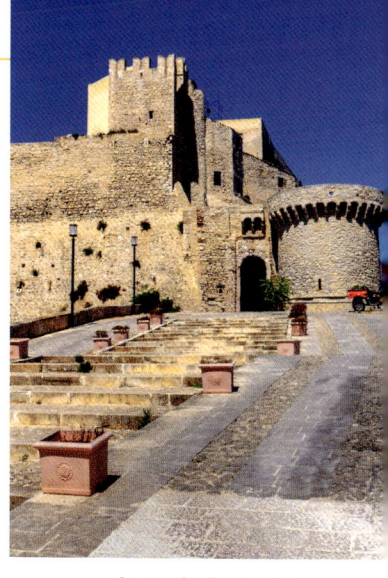

San Nicola's battlements

Benedictine monks founded the Abbey on San Nicola in 1010 which by the thirteenth century had amassed great wealth. In 1412 it was fortified to withstand attacks from the Turks. In 1782 the abbey was suppressed by King Ferdinand IV of Naples and transformed into a penal colony. From the port of San Nicola take the steep path up to the battlements leading to the graceful Romanesque-style Church of Santa Maria a Mare. Founded in 1045 and remodelled over the centuries, the church has a beautiful portal, an eleventh- to twelfth-century mosaic pavement and a wooden Byzantine cross. Beyond the church you can wander among cloisters, overgrown ruins and ancient Greek tombs, all the while enjoying panoramic views of the islands.

San Domino

The largest and greenest of the islands, San Domino lacks the old-world charm of San Nicola but offers some beautiful secluded coves, a fine white-sand beach and a handful of hotels, villas and restaurants. The Benedictine monks called this island Paradise Orchard thanks to its fertility, profusion of flowers and shady woods. From its fragrant pine-clad slopes there are fine views of the pristine seas.

Il Tavoliere

In stark contrast to the mountainous Gargano Peninsula are the vast, flat wheatlands of **Il Tavoliere** ❼ stretching west from the Gargano massif to the foothills of the Apennines. This is also an industrial area and the towns have limited appeal to tourists. **Foggia** ❽, the capital of the eponymous province, is rarely visited by tourists but retains a Romanesque cathedral, remodelled in the eighteenth century. **Lucera** ❾ has Puglia's only Gothic cathedral

---

DIVING AND BOAT TRIPS

The unbelievably translucent waters around the Tremiti Islands offer some of the best diving and snorkelling in southern Italy. The uninhabited and protected little island of Capraia, with its quiet coves, is one of the best diving spots, particularly at Punta Secca and Cala dei Turchi. On a 14m (46ft) -deep seabed near the islet a statue of Padre Pio (see page 39) was submerged in 1998. The small boats which take tourists around the islands stop here so they can dive down to see the statue. However, unless the sea is really calm, it's not always easy for the boatman to locate the statue. The boats also skirt the craggy limestone cliffs of San Domino, which are pitted with fascinating caves. One of the most famous is the Grotta delle Viole, where in spring the rocks are covered by caper flowers that look like wild violets (*viole*). Inside the water's hues and clarity defy description.

Cycling in Il Tavoliere

in southern Italy, as well as the ruins of Frederick II's largest castle; **Troia** ⑩, the most attractive town of the region, has a remarkable cathedral with a successful fusion of Pisan-Romanesque architecture and Byzantine Saracen-inspired ornament.

Puglia Imperiale

Highlights
- **Castel del Monte**, see page 44
- **The coast**, see page 45
- **Barletta**, see page 45
- **Canne della Battaglia**, see page 46
- **Canosa di Puglia**, see page 47
- **Trani**, see page 49

The region extending west from Bari is known as Puglia Imperiale, on account of the legacy of Frederick II, the dominant figure in Puglia's long and varied history. This is a land of castles, cathedrals and historic cities. The Castel del Monte, dominating the countryside around Andria, is a supreme example of the 29 castles which Frederick built in Puglia. Along the coast the seaside stunner is Trani, known as 'the pearl of Puglia' and boasting a dazzling white cathedral suspended between a sky and a sea that vie for brilliant blues.

A car is a best way to explore the region, particularly if you intend to visit Castel del Monte.

Castel del Monte, an octagonal masterpiece

Castel del Monte

Dominating the landscape, on a 540m (1,771ft)-high rocky peak, stands Frederick II's stronghold and retreat: the medieval **Castel del Monte** ⓫ (https://musei puglia.cultura.gov.it/musei/castel-del-monte/; charge, fee-paying shuttle service from car park to castle). The imposing structure had a unique design for the time: a perfectly proportioned octagonal plan with octagonal towers at each angle – possibly the influence of Middle Eastern architecture.

The monument has always been a puzzle for historians. Its thick 26m (85ft)-high walls and towers suggest it was part of Frederick's network of strategically placed defensive castles, yet it has no drawbridge, moat, arrow slits, dungeons for prisoners or other fortress features and the large marble rooms with mosaics, paintings and tapestries (treasures that were looted long ago) are more like those you would find in a lavish royal residence. Some experts suggest that the design was inspired by astronomy, a science known to have fascinated the cultured Frederick.

> **NOTES**
>
> If you're in Italy you may well have a picture of the Castel del Monte in your pocket. The castle is depicted on the reverse side of the Italian one euro cent coin.

The castle served as a refuge for the noble families of nearby **Andria** ⓬ during the plague of 1665 and was later abandoned, becoming a hideout for brigands and political exiles. The state bought it in 1876, and three years later began a forty-year restoration programme. The site was awarded UNESCO World Heritage status in 1996. The interior is spartan but there are audio guides to help you imagine the castle in former times.

The coast

As you come south from the Gargano Peninsula the coast is flat with extensive salt flats at Margherita di Savoia. Producing over five million tons of salt a year these are among the largest in Europe. The protected wetlands along this coastline are of ornithological interest and have one of the largest colonies of pink flamingos in Europe.

Barletta

The first main town you come to is **Barletta** ⓭, a busy port and industrial centre. The town retains an historic centre with a handsome castle built by Frederick II, a Romanesque cathedral and, most famously, the **Colossus**, a bronze statue of a Byzantine

FREDERICK II

As well as being King of Germany and Holy Roman Emperor, Frederick of Hohenstaufen (1194–1250) acquired the titles of King of Sicily, King of Italy, Holy Roman Emperor and King of Jerusalem. His mother was Constance of Altavilla, later to become Queen of Sicily, his father Henry VI of the Hohenstaufen dynasty. At the age of four Frederick became an orphan and was placed under the protection of Pope Innocent III. Styled '*Stupor Mundi*' (Wonder of the World), he took control of southern Italy in 1220 and became the most significant political and intellectual figure of thirteenth-century Europe. An enlightened ruler who waged a bitter and ultimately unsuccessful feud with the Papacy, he was also an avid sportsman whose brilliant treatise on falconry still ranks among the most accurate descriptions of the subject. Influenced by Arabic and Jewish learning and imbued with the eastern spirit of his age as well as the pragmatism of the Norman rulers who preceded him, Frederick brought to bear a unique unifying spirit in Sicily and southern Italy. Through his court he nurtured philosophy, poetry, mathematics and the natural sciences. In Puglia he struck such a chord with the people that he was nicknamed '*Puer Apuliae*' or Son of Apulia. Frederick left his mark on castles across the region and in particular on Castel del Monte, his own masterly fusion of poetry and mathematics in stone.

emperor, more remarkable for its size (over 5m/16ft high) and age (over 1,500 years old) than any aesthetic merit. It was reputedly stolen by Venetians from Constantinople but it was reported that the boat sank and the statue was washed ashore at Barletta. Behind the statue rises Barletta's most important church of all, the **Chiesa del Santo Sepolcro**, which is a remodelled Romanesque church that played an important role during the Crusades.

Canne della Battaglia

A hill in the lower Ofanto valley, inland from Barletta, was the site of one of the most pivotal battles in classical history and one of the worst defeats ever suffered by the Roman army. Having already defeated two Roman armies during the Second Punic War, Hannibal based himself in the town of Cannae, making it his base to conquer southern Italy. On August 2, 216 BC, an army of 86,000 Roman troops faced 40,000 Carthaginians at the site which is now called the **Canne della Battaglia** ⓮. Hannibal's brilliant use of tactics led to the virtual annihilation of the Roman fighting force. Seventy thousand Romans were killed, 4,500 taken prisoner. Nothing remains of the battleground, but the site is protected as the **Antiquarium** and **Parco Archeologico di Canne della Battaglia** (https://museipuglia.cultura.gov.it/musei/museo-e-parco-archeologico-canne-della-battaglia/; charge). The new Antiquarium documents the history of Cannae from Prehistory to the Middle Ages, with emphasis on the historical battle while the Archeological Park reveals the remains of an ancient Daunian settlement, along with Roman, early Christian and medieval remains.

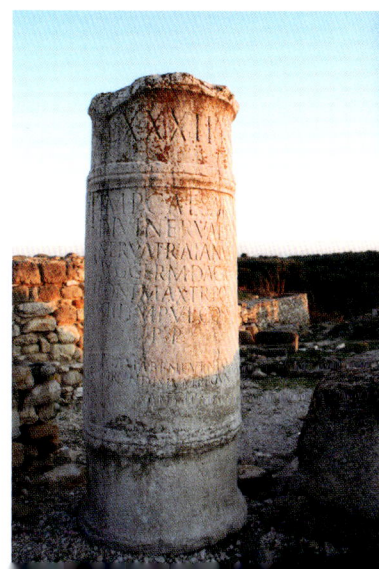

Canne della Battaglia ruins

Canosa di Puglia

Further archeological finds can be seen at **Canosa di Puglia** ⓯ 13km (8 miles) southwest of Canne della Battaglia, and nicknamed Little Rome because of its seven hills. Although a rather dreary town today it was a major city in Roman times. Archeological finds,

WHERE TO SHOOT THE BEST PICTURES

The photogenic **landscape of the Gargano promontory**, with its rocky coast, makes for scenic photographs, especially if you stand at the base of the mountains at noon when there are no shadows. When driving south **on the coastal route to Bari**, get snapping from the car as you pass through the pretty towns and villages with their markets and lively seafronts. You'll need to be on a boat to photograph **the sea grottoes and cliffs of Santa Maria di Leuca** at their best, but it's definitely worth it.

For urban shots, get morning shots of the **Baroque Piazza Sant'Oronzo in Lecce** (try different perspectives to include more or less cobblestones) or of one of the many **piazzas of Taranto**, for example the majestic Piazza Marinai d'Italia at sunset when the lamp posts have just turned on, or Piazza Ebalia in the afternoon. Bari bustles with life around lunchtime, and the **Città Vecchia at the end of Corso Cavour** is the best spot to capture the in action. For surreal landscapes, head to the **trulli town of Alberobello** around midday and take pictures with a couple of *trulli* in the background. Walk around **Matera** and you'll find many incredible snapshot opportunities, but for a panoramic shot of the entire Sassi scenery you'll have to go to the Belvedere Murgia Timone, which can be reached by car, followed by a short walk.

dispersed across the city and often tricky to access without a guide, include the Hypogea Lagrasta, a rock-hewn complex of underground tombs. The largest of the three hypogea has nine rooms and fragments of frescoes.

Cattedrale di San Sabino

Treasures within the town's five-domed **Cattedrale di San Sabino** include an eleventh-century pulpit, the early twelfth-century tomb of Bohemond I, Prince of Taranto, with magnificent bronze doors and the oldest bishop's throne in Apulia, carved by the eleventh-century sculptor, Romualdo. The animal carvings show traces of

Arab influence, and the throne has been compared to an Islamic chess piece.

Trani

Following the fall of Canosa to the Saracens in the ninth century, the fishing port of **Trani** ⓰ expanded and became one of the most important Italian trading centres, rivalling Bari as a commercial port. The iconic site is its cathedral, but this is just one of many monuments in Trani's beautifully restored historic centre. The town has a marked air of prosperity with streets of glistening marble cobbles, elegant boutiques, finely preserved *palazzi* and fashionable cafés and bars.

The intricately carved door of the Cattedrale di San Nicola Pellegrino

Cattedrale di San Nicola Pellegrino

The town's dominant and most dramatically located monument is the **Cattedrale di San Nicola Pellegrino** (www.cattedraletrani.it; charge only for campanile), one of the finest examples of Apulian-Romanesque architecture. It was founded at the end of the eleventh century to house the remains of a young Greek pilgrim called Nicola who died in Trani. The portal is adorned with finely carved sculptures and frames bronze doors with 32 impressive reliefs. The restored original doors, carved by the twelfth-century sculptor Barisano of Trani, who also cast the bronze doors of Ravello's Cathedral, are preserved inside the church.

The interior is divided into an upper and lower church. The upper was restored to its Romanesque design from the elaborate Baroque modelling it was given in 1837: it is narrow, lofty and light, bare of ornament, with two tiers and a beamed ceiling. Below is a crypt with a forest of pillars and a lower church adorned with fourteenth- and fifteenth-century frescoes. For those prepared to climb 258 steps there are fine views from the top of the 60m (170ft)-high Campanile.

Trani's elegant port

Castello Svevo

Guarding the seashore just to the west of the cathedral piazza is the **Castello Svevo**, (Swabian Castle; http://

The Villa Communale, Trani's green oasis

cultura.gov.it/luogo/castello-svevo-di-trani). The castle was part of Frederick II's intense programme of demolition, restoration and building of fortifications, transforming Puglia from a land of cathedrals to a land of castles. Built in 1233–49, with later alterations and heavy restoration, the castle has a square design, four large corner towers and a moat which once joined the sea. It served as a prison from the nineteenth century until 1975. Today it's a tourist sight and cultural centre but apart from a small museum, with finds from the restoration work, there is little to see inside.

Jewish Quarter
A stroll through the narrow alleys of Trani's historic centre will reveal medieval churches, handsome *palazzi* and two synagogues. Under Frederick II a large Jewish community flourished in Trani

Bari Vecchia backstreet

and the city had four active synagogues, but by 1380 all four had been converted to churches, and the remaining Jews were forced to convert to Christianity. Two synagogues survive. The **Scola Grande** on Via La Giudea (the main street of the ancient Ghetto), later converted into the Chiesa di Sant'Anna, now houses the Jewish section of Trani's Diocesan Museum. Just to the south the **Scola Nova** ('New Synagogue') became the Chiesa di Santa Maria in Scolanova. It was deconsecrated and returned to the Jewish community in 2004, when the Jewish community was formally recreated. Today's tiny community consists of the descendants of the Jews who were forcibly converted during the Inquisition and of those who for centuries had to conceal their Jewish identity.

Chiesa di Ognissanti
A two-minute walk to the east, with its entrance on Via Ognissanti, is the simple and evocative **Chiesa di Ognissanti** (free). Founded in the twelfth century this recently restored church was said to have formerly been a Knights Templar church. Don't miss the lovely facade at the east end with the bell tower and three semicircular apses facing Trani's elegant little **port**. By day this is a picturesque scene of colourful fishing boats and yachts, whilst after dark it's the

lively scene of the *passeggiata* (evening stroll) and abuzz with café and restaurant life. If you walk all the way round you come to the **Villa Comunale**, Trani's delightful public gardens.

Bari and beyond

Highlights
- **Bari**, see page 53
- **Polignano a Mare**, see page 57

A major trading port since ancient times, Bari reached its zenith in the medieval era and by the eleventh century was the most important Adriatic port. Today it is the capital of Puglia, the main point of arrival by air to the region and still a busy port with ferries serving Greece, Croatia and Albania. Tourists who arrive here rarely make time to see the city, unaware that it is no longer a down-at-heel port. Reinvented Bari has become a more welcoming, cosmopolitan city offering chic shopping and lively nightlife as well as history, culture and a fascinating historic centre. It even has its cuisine, *cucina barese,* with some great street food and seafood restaurants. Although the city is far safer than it used to be it's still wise to keep an eye on valuables as you stroll around the streets.

Bari is the gateway to Adriatic resorts and towns of central Puglia; it is also only an hour's drive from Matera in Basilicata (see page 88). A favourite excursion for the Baresi is the fashionable resort of Polignano a Mare, 34km (21 miles) south of the city (see page 57).

Bari
The city of **Bari** ⓱ consists of Bari Vecchia, or Old Bari, and the Città Nuova, or modern quarter, laid out on a grid plan with wide, straight avenues. The latter is the financial and administrative centre and the location of museums, theatres, concert halls and the

University of Bari Aldo Moro. Via Sparano is home to the famous fashion labels, Corso Cavour and Via Manzoni is home to the cheaper stores.

Bari Vecchia

Packed on a promontory between the old and new ports, **Bari Vecchia** is an atmospheric maze of medieval alleys, small courtyards, shrines and churches. The old town can be covered on foot; alternatively there are bicycles, Segways and scooters to rent – or tuk-tuks at the ready if you want a personal tour. Meandering around on foot it is easy to get lost in the tangle of streets but you are never far from a landmark. Delis and eateries proliferate: hole-in-the-wall grocery stores sell nuts and spices, small tavernas serve bowls of *cozze* (mussels) and home-made pasta while grandmas can be glimpsed through doorways hand-rolling *orecchiette* (ear-shaped pasta) or in the alleys or squares frying *sgagliozze* (squares of polenta). The Baresi love their sushi and at the fish market you can see them opening freshly caught sea urchins and mussels, sprinkling them with lemon juice and washing them down with a bottle of chilled Peroni.

On the western edge is the vast **Castello Normanno Svevo** Ⓐ (Norman Swabian Castle; www.cultura.gov.it/luogo/castello-svevo-di-bari; charge). One of Frederick II's many fortifications, this was built in 1233–40 over the ruins of a Norman fortress, from which it retains two towers, later embellished and converted into a splendid dwelling by the Aragonese. To access the castle cross the bridge over the moat that is now a public garden. Unlike most Puglian castles there is a fair amount to see inside, including temporary exhibitions, archeological remains, ceramics and the particularly appealing Gallery of Plaster Casts, exhibiting reproductions of medieval and post-medieval architectural features, including capitals, corbels and gargoyles, all from major monuments and museums in Puglia.

On Piazza dell'Odegitria you're unlikely to miss the **Cattedrale di San Sabino** ❸ (free). The majestic white facade, with a soaring belltower, dominates the square and looks particularly stunning against a blue sky. The church was dedicated to St Sabinus, a bishop of Canosa, whose remains were brought here in the ninth century, and which today lie in the crypt. The church was transformed from its Baroque excess to the simple style of the original Puglian-Romanesque. Below the cathedral the **Museo del Succorpo della Cattedrale** (charge) is a hidden gem, retaining the remains of earlier buildings, including a medieval Christian basilica on the same site. On show are some remarkable mosaics, tombs and part of a Roman road – all with good explanations in English.

Polignano a Mare, a cliff-diver's paradise

North of the cathedral in the heart of old Bari rises the austere, almost fortress-like **Basilica di San Nicola** C (www.basilicasannicola.it; charge), one of the first great Norman churches in Southern Italy. In 1087, 62 sailors from Bari left for Myra in Lycia (present-day Turkey) and purloined the relics of bishop Nicholas. A Byzantine edifice in Bari was transformed into a magnificent basilica, construction of which lasted for over a century, and the saint's relics were housed in the beautiful crypt – where they still lie. For centuries the basilica has been a destination for pilgrims from all over the Christian world who come to see the shrine containing the remains. San Nicola has always overshadowed the city's cathedral since at the time of construction the importance of a town was determined by the relics it held, gained at any cost and by any means. Within the enclosure of the San Nicola Citadel lies the pretty Romanesque **Chiesa di San Gregorio** D, the oldest consecrated church in Bari, dating back to the tenth century. North of San Nicola lies the newly-reopened **Museo Archeologico di Santa Scolastica** E (www.museoarcheologicosantascolastica.it; charge). Set in the ancient monastery of Santa Scolastica the museum is incorporated within a sixteenth-century bastion, the gateway to Old Bari for those arriving at the city by

Ruins at Egnazia

sea. A modern museum, with a multimedia route, it has beautifully arranged exhibits from Puglian prehistory to the Bronze Age, along with jewellery and other treasures from the Greek, Byzantine and medieval periods.

In the evenings life focuses on **Piazza Mercantile** �, a handsome square fringed by open-air restaurants and overlooked by the Palazzo del Sedile and the Colonna della Giustizia (Column of Justice) where debtors were exposed to public ridicule. The adjoining Piazza del Ferrarese is home to the tourist office.

> **NOTES**
>
> If you're a fan of the famous Italian song *'Volare'* don't miss the statue of its singer, Domenico Modugno, Polignano's favourite son. He stands with arms outstretched on the seafront just west of Cala Porto. He enjoyed jumping from the nearby cliffs into the sea – which is said to have inspired *'Volare'* (to fly).

Polignano a Mare

A favourite excursion for the Baresi is the photogenic and fashionable resort of **Polignano a Mare** �, 34km (21 miles) south of the city. The town perches high on the cliffs above the waters of the Adriatic – so high in fact that the resort is now a venue for the Red Bull Cliff Diving World Series, whose elite cliff-divers compete from heights of up to 27m (89ft) in chosen places around the globe. Once a year the cliff-divers gather here, accessing platforms up to this height through a private house in the cliffs. Around seventy thousand fans flock to Polignano to watch the event while at other times of the year adrenalin junkies enjoy jumping into the water from the top of the rocks.

Twenty years ago Polignano a Mare was almost derelict, a coastal town in a poor agricultural region. Now it is one of the best-known spots on the Adriatic: a thriving resort with 85,000 annual visitors, a lively restaurant and bar scene, spectacular boat trips along the cave-riddled cliffs and entertaining rickshaw rides with food and wine tasting. The historic centre, built on the clifftops, is small but appealing with its little whitewashed alleys, narrow flights of steps and terraces with stunning views of the sea and coastline. When the wind is up, this is a popular spot to watch the waves crash against the cliffs. Just below the old town lies Cala Porto, a cove flanked by cliffs where the sea is crystal clear. It's ideal out of season but there's not a spare inch on the pebble beach in July and August.

A walk west along the cliffs will bring you to the **Fondazione Museo Pino Pascali** (www.fondazionepascali.it; charge), a striking

The weird and wonderful Grotte di Castellana

museum of contemporary art in a converted abattoir overlooking the sea. The museum was officially opened in 2012 and displays works by artist, sculptor and set-designer, Pino Pascali (1935–68) who was born in Bari and lived for some time in Polignano a Mare. He died tragically in a motorbike accident in Rome at the age of 33. The museum also exhibits contemporary works by other Puglian artists and hosts temporary exhibitions, events, seminars and workshops.

A short drive along the coast brings you to the city of **Monopoli** ⓭, with a large, lavish cathedral, a seafront castle, a fishing port and good beaches. **Egnazia** ⓴, 18km (11 miles) to the south, was the site of a fourth-century Greco-Roman or Greco-Massapian town, and preserves ruins of foundations of houses, roads and tombs. It's a pretty setting by the sea but you need a good imagination to envisage this one-time key settlement on the Via Appia. It helps to visit the **Museo Archeologico Nazionale di Egnazia** (http://museipuglia.cultura.gov.it; charge), which has been renovated and expanded to include a section about the town's relation to the sea, located in the museum's basements. For most tourists the area is best known for the deluxe *Borgo Egnazia* (see page 101), where Justin Timberlake and Jessica Biel married in 2012.

Valle d'Itria

Highlights
- **Grotte di Castellana**, see page 60
- **Alberobello**, see page 61
- **Locorotondo**, see page 62
- **Martina Franca**, see page 63
- **Cisternino**, see page 65
- **Ostuni**, see page 66

Spreading over the provinces of Bari, Brindisi and Taranto, the Valle d'Itria is best known for the white cities that crown its hilltops and for the distinctive dwellings known as *trulli*. These small, conical-roofed, whitewashed houses have dotted the landscape for centuries. The town of Alberobello, a UNESCO World Heritage Site, has them en masse, but you can also see them in their natural surroundings, among the vines, olives and almonds, on the fertile plain between Locorotondo and Martina Franca. Fans of these hobbit-style houses can stay in a *trullo* hotel – or pray in a *trullo* church. There is also the option of staying in one of the region's many *masserie,* the fortified farmhouses, many of which have been converted into boutique hotels or spa resorts.

Grotte di Castellana

In 1938 a 3km (2 mile)-long labyrinth of underground caves and chambers was discovered 65m (213ft) below ground level near the town of Castellana, north of Alberobello. The **Grotte di Castellana** ㉑ (Piazzale Anelli; www.grottedicastellana.it; charge), often cited as the most spectacular caves in Italy, have remarkable stalactite and stalagmites, and weird and wonderful rock formations such

---

TRULLI EXTRAORDINARY

Some sources maintain that the original *trulli* were built by Byzantine monks as early as the eighth century, others that they were primitive tombs and that the various symbols on the roofs have magic, Christian or pagan significance. However, some experts think the explanation is more simple – they were built from the early sixteenth century by shepherds and farmers with stones cleared from the fields. There is also a theory that the ancient building style was revived to thwart the tax collectors of the Kingdom of the Two Sicilies: the dwellings had dry stone walls so could be dismantled quickly before the tax collector arrived – then later rebuilt. The oldest *trulli* still standing date from the seventeenth century. Out in the country you can find *trulli* (and *trulli*-inspired) farms, barns, grain silos and even petrol stations.

as the Cyclops, Capitoline She-Wolf, Pillars of Hercules, Cathedral of Milan and Tower of Pisa. The chambers are reached by lift and visited either on a 1km (0.5 mile) 50-minute tour or the more spectacular two-hour 3km (2 mile) tour which includes the staggeringly beautiful **Grotta Bianca**, an alabaster cavern with cream-coloured, needle-sharp stalactites. The temperature is around 18°C (64°F) all year so you may need an extra layer of clothing – as well as comfortable shoes. On Speleonight Tours you can listen to the night sounds of the caves and watch the creepy crawlies that populate them. From April to December the biggest of the caves is the setting of the underground theatrical show, *Hell in the Cave,* inspired by Dante's Inferno.

Picture-perfect Locorotondo

Alberobello

Few places in Puglia have better signage than **Alberobello** ㉒, where tourists flock to see the fairy-tale forest of *trulli*. The old part of town has around 1,500 of these quaint, beehive-shaped buildings. Brown signs lead you to the well worn **Rione Monti** street in the upper part of town, flanked by shops selling mini *trulli*, olive oil, crafts and multi-coloured creamy liqueurs. *Trulli* owners will invite you in for free tasting of local products. The street climbs up to the Church of Sant'Antonio, also a *trullo* but a relatively modern one,

Piazza Plebiscito, Martina Franca

dating from 1927. The less touristy and more tranquil part of the Trulli Zone is the **Rione Aia Piccola** quarter on the eastern side. Many of the dwellings here are family homes and not given over to tourism. The only two-storey *trullo* is the **Trullo Sovrano** (Piazza Sacramento 10; www.trullosovrano.eu; charge) on the northern edge of town, now a museum, furnished as it would have been when occupied in the eighteenth century.

Locorotondo

One of the most picturesque towns of Puglia, **Locorotondo** ㉓ (Round Place) takes its name from the setting. Less well-known than nearby Alberobello, it is a white hilltop town laid out in concentric circles. The dazzling white houses and the vast dome and lofty bell-tower of the neoclassical Chiesa di San Giorgio can be seen from afar and from the town itself there are fine views out over the vineyards of the Itria Valley. The vines produce white, red and rosé wines but the town is best known for the white Locorotondo DOP.

Once fortified with walls and keeps, the historical centre retains some fine *palazzi* and churches, quiet courtyards and winding cobbled alleys. Everything is daubed in dazzling whitewash, contrasting with the lush green of potted plants and brilliant reds of geraniums or hibiscus. It is a lovely spot for a stroll, and has some tempting little tavernas and places for *degustazione* (tasting) of the local specialities: *salumi*, cheeses, olive oil and *taralli* (round biscuits).

Martina Franca

The largest and liveliest town of the Valle d'Itria is **Martina Franca** ㉔, renowned for its Baroque architecture. The site was settled in the tenth century by fugitives from Taranto escaping Saracen invaders but was largely developed in the fourteenth century

CAPOCOLLO DI MARTINA FRANCA

Carnivores shouldn't miss out on Capocollo di Martina Franca, a speciality of the region since the eighteenth century. This sweet, delicately smoked, cured ham was awarded 'Slow Food' protected status. The pork, which comes from prized pigs of the Murgia region, is rubbed with salt, pepper and spices and left for fifteen days. After being marinated in herbs and *Vin Cotto* (a 'cooked' wine, slowly simmered until thick and syrupy), it is stuffed into a natural casing and left for about a fortnight. It is then smoked with the bark of oak, almond husks and Mediterranean herbs and left to cure for at least three months. The meat is often served with other salamis from the region or as a filler for *panini* with Pecorino or Canestrato cheese. A bottle of Primitivo wine is the perfect accompaniment.

when Philip of Anjou granted it fiscal exemptions – hence the Franca (Free) part of the name (Martina comes from San Martino, the patron saint). The charm of the town lies in narrow streets, fine churches and graceful eighteenth-century town houses, with Baroque features and beautiful wrought-iron balconies. The town is lively and civilised, known for its chic shops and gastronomy, based on superb cold meats (see box), cheeses and pasta. There is also a local white wine, Martina Franca, which comes either still or sparkling (*spumante*).

The spacious tree-lined **Piazza XX Settembre**, the town's main square, is a popular rendezvous and the venue of the *passeggiata*. Heralding the old city is the triumphal arch known as the **Porto Santo Stefano** (also known as the Arco di Sant'Antonio). Just to the right of it is the tourist office which provides a free map, suggesting five walking itineraries and no less than 53 cultural attractions. Beyond the arch, overlooking the Piazza Roma and the Dolphin Fountain, you are unlikely to miss the grand **Palazzo Ducale** (Ducal Palace; charge only for royal apartments). On the site of the fourteenth century Orsini castle, this seventeenth-century palace was built for the Caracciolo dukes who ruled here in the city's heyday. It is now the town hall but you can visit the royal apartments on the *piano nobile,* hung with Murano glass chandeliers and adorned with Rococo murals (1776) by Domenico Carella. These depict the ducal family in scenes from Roman and Greek mythology and from the Bible.

The Corso Vittorio Emanuele, lined by chic shops, leads to **Piazza Plebiscito**, dwarfed by the lofty and undulating Baroque facade of the **Chiesa di San Martino**. A sculptural group over the main portal shows St Martin, the city's patron saint, swinging a sword and sharing his cloak with a beggar. The church has a richly adorned interior with a profusion of coloured marble. Beyond it, the Palazzo dell'Università with stone carvings is flanked by a Baroque clock tower and in the next square a lovely Baroque *portico* shelters a couple of the city's many restaurants. At the end of Via Garibaldi brown signs point you left and right in the direction of nine monuments, taking you along winding narrow alleys to the edge of the walled city.

Cisternino

On the edge of the Valle d'Itria, **Cisternino** ㉕ is a delightful little town of whitewashed houses perched on a hilltop and surrounded by olive groves. The old quarter has a typically Mediterranean look with houses built around an inner courtyard with outer staircases leading to the upper floors. The town has more than its fair share of family-run, simple trattorias, many of them meat-focused, though

A snapshot of trulli heaven

Ostuni's old quarter

like elsewhere in the area, many of them are slowly being replaced by more fancy eateries to cater for a more sophisticated type of tourism. The town is known as *la città della bombetta*, the *bombetta* being parcels of meat, usually thin slices of pork filled with cheese and spices, then rolled up and cooked on a grill or in the oven (or taken home to cook). Accompaniments such as bread and wine are usually on hand.

Ostuni

The best known of the region's '*città bianche*' (white cities), **Ostuni** ㉖ stretches dramatically over three hilltops, overlooking plains of olive groves. The historic centre, surrounded by city walls, has steep winding alleys, fine Baroque buildings and a jumbled pyramid of chalk-white, flat-roofed houses.

The focus of town life is the **Piazza della Libertà**, overlooked by the stately Municipio (Town Hall) and the **Chiesa di San Francesco** which at first glance looks Renaisssance but was almost entirely rebuilt. The marble statues of St Francis of Assisi and St Anthony of Padua in the niches on the facade for example are twentieth century. At the far end a 20m (65ft) decorative **Obelisco di Sant'Oronzo** is topped by a statue of the city's patron saint, Sant'Oronzo. He was credited with ending the plague in the city in 1656 and every year is honoured with a three-day festival in

Ostuni (August 25–27). From Piazza della Libertà the cobbled Via Cattedrale climbs up towards the historic centre, and is flanked by shops selling local crafts and gastronomic delights. En route stop at the **Museo Civico**, which is also known as the **Museo di Civiltà Preclassiche della Murgia Meridionale** (Museum of Preclassical Civilisation of Southern Murgia; www.ostunimuseo.it/museo-civico; currently closed for restoration) within the mid-eighteenth-century Church of San Vito Martire (known as Le Monacelle). The most famous of its archeological exhibits is a 27,000-year-old skeleton of a young woman known as Delia which was discovered in 1991 in a grotto close to Ostuni. It was surrounded by the skeletons and teeth of animals which would have been hunted by her

Waterfront restaurant in Brindisi

tribe. But the most remarkable discovery was the fact that she was pregnant and bore the skeleton of the dead foetus in her womb. The remains were carefully removed from the cave and they were taken for safekeeping to Ostuni's museum.

At the heart of Ostuni's old quarter and dominating the tallest hill is the late Gothic **Cattedrale** (1435–95). It has an elegant and unusual facade, with its pointy top, curves and magnificent rose window, decorated with zoomorphical and biblical scenes. The Latin-cross interior was completely remodelled in the eighteenth century, with Baroque chapels on the sides. The Palazzo Vescovile (Bishop's Palace) and the Palazzo del Seminario, with an arched loggia connecting the two, look on to the same square as the church, creating a theatre-stage effect. The narrow streets beyond, with Baroque portals, *palazzi* and small squares, are well worth exploring.

The Salento

Highlights
- **Brindisi**, see page 69
- **Lecce**, see page 71
- **The Grecia Salentina**, see page 76
- **Otranto**, see page 78
- **South from Otranto**, see page 81
- **Santa Maria di Leuca**, see page 83
- **Gallipoli**, see page 83
- **Taranto**, see page 85

The Salentine Peninsula or Salento is framed by the Ionian and Adriatic seas and stretches to the most southerly part of Italy's heel. It is famed for its sun-baked beaches and sees relatively few tourists outside the high season. But Salento also has plenty of cultural interest, embracing the beautiful Baroque city of Lecce, the lovely coastal towns of Otranto and Gallipoli, the 'Greek' towns south of Lecce as well as sleepy southern villages. Life is relaxed and slow-paced here. Nothing is contrived or picture perfect – which of course is all part of its charm.

Brindisi

Historic **Brindisi** ㉗ has been a busy port since ancient times. In Roman times it was the most important port in southern Italy, and was linked to Rome by the 350 mile (563km)-long Appian Way (Via Antica) which facilitated trade and travel to Greece and the east. Today Brindisi teems with travellers throughout the summer, most en route to Greece. It is not a city where many tourists choose to

Brindisi's Duomo

stay but it has a handful of historic sights, and the seafront with its palms and white canopied cafés is a pleasant place to stroll. Across the harbour rises the **Monumento Al Marinaio d'Italia** (Monument to Italian Sailors; free), a soaring, rudder-shaped tower in memory of fallen soldiers between Unification and 1933 – when the monument was erected. It is built in typical fascist style and has panoramic views of the city and harbour from the top.

From the waterfront a sweeping flight of steps, known as the **Scalinata Virgiliana**, ascends to the **Roman Column**, marking the terminus of the Via Appia. One of the two columns collapsed in 1528 and was taken to Lecce where it now supports a bronze statue of the city's patron saint, St Oronzo. As you look at the column with your back to the sea, the slightly derelict house to your left with a modern ground floor is, according to some historians, the house where Virgil spent the last days of his life.

An archway leads to the **Duomo** (Cathedral) where Frederick II married his second wife Yolande in 1225. The church was destroyed by an earthquake in 1743 and rebuilt. The nearby **Museo Archeologico Provinciale Ribezzo** (http://cartapulia.it/dettaglio?id=129434; free) has three floors of archeological treasures, from fine Attic ceramics to an exceptional collection of Hellenistic bronzes which were discovered at the bottom of the sea near Brindisi harbour in the early 1990s.

The tourist office is located on Via Duomo in the beautiful **Palazzo Granafei-Nervegna**, part of which houses the huge capital that topped one of the Roman Columns. It is kept here to preserve it from sea-salt erosion (the one on the column is a copy). At this level you can appreciate all the detail including tritons and male and female sea-gods. West of the palace the **Tempio di San Giovanni al Sepolcro** (free) on the eponymous piazza is a gem of a church, constructed on the lines of the Holy Sepulchre in Jerusalem. It was built at the behest of Norman prince Bohemond who wanted to show his gratitude for the success of the First

Crusade, of which he had been one of the leaders. It has a fine Norman portal and a lovely, intimate interior with thirteenth- to fifteenth-century frescoes.

Lecce

Lecce ㉘ was once a key crossroads of the Mediterranean, coveted by foreign invaders over the centuries. Today it's best known as the Baroque gem of Puglia. The exuberant decorative style known as 'Lecce Baroque' began in the mid-seventeenth century and flourished for about sixty years. In a land of stout Norman castles and restrained Romanesque churches, the city of fanciful facades at every turn comes as a glorious surprise. Aided by the softness

Lecce's Roman amphitheatre

> **NOTES**
>
> After a day taking in Lecce's lavish architecture, you might like to try a very apt local speciality: *sagne n'cannulate*. This pasta dish, traditionally served with a simple tomato and cheese sauce, is made with long twisted ribbons of pasta which mimic the city's swirling architecture.

of the local limestone, the stonemasons let their chisels run wild. Balconies are supported by grinning caryatids, classical columns are festooned with foliage, window frames are laden with swags of fruit while portals drip with trophies and crests. The main architect was Giuseppe Zimbalo, familiarly known as 'Lo Zingarello', the Little Gypsy. The city has over forty churches (along with countless Baroque *palazzi* and a castle), of which only the main ones in the centre are covered below.

Lecce is also a university town, with a lively cultural programme and some excellent restaurants. It is known for its cuisine and cookery schools where you can learn how to make local pasta from scratch and visit markets and food and wine producers.

Piazza Sant'Oronzo

In the heart of Lecce is **Piazza Sant'Oronzo**, whose history spans two thousand years. St Oronzo, the city's patron saint, blesses the city from atop the soaring Roman column which was donated by Brindisians in the belief that Oronzo had saved their city from the plague. Below lie the remains of a **Roman amphitheatre** dating from the second century AD and seating around 25,000. It was only rediscovered during works in the early twentieth century when a large part of the piazza was destroyed for the construction of the Banca d'Italia. Mussolini resurrected the theatre ruins (the upper level was lost though the pillars still stand) but also added fascist architecture resulting in the hotchpotch of styles in the square you see today. The amphitheatre was opened in 2000 as a concert venue after a six-year restoration but is now roped off (but visible) to prevent any further deterioration. Finds from the amphitheatre can be seen at the city's archeological museum, the **Museo Provinciale Sigismondo Castromediano** (Viale Gallipoli 28; http://cultura.gov.it/luogo/museo-sigismondo-castromediano; free). The unusual Renaissance pavilion or **Sedile** on the Piazza Sant'Oronzo has variously served as the seat of the mayor, the Town Council, the National Guard and the municipal museum. Much of it was demolished by Mussolini and today it houses the tourist information office (www.visitlecce.eu).

Basilica di Santa Croce

The most complete expression of Leccese Baroque is the **Basilica di Santa Croce** (Via Umberto I; https://basilicasantacrocelecce.it; charge) just to the north of Piazza Sant'Oronzo. The medieval cathedral which formerly stood here was demolished and rebuilt by Zimbalo. Looking at the wildly elaborate facade, with its large and lavish rose window and profusion of *putti*, strange beasts, sea gods and caryatids, it comes as no surprise to learn that the church took nearly 150 years to build (1549–1695). The interior, where the predominant style is late Renaissance,

In the streets of Lecce

Abbazia di Santa Maria di Cerrate

is restrained in comparison to the facade. Zimbalo also built the adjoining Baroque Convento dei Celestini, now the Palazzo della Provincia, occupied by Government offices. Just south of the Basilica on the site of the old synagogue is the **Museo Ebraico** (Jewish Museum, Via Umberto I 9; www.museoebraicolecce.it; charge) focuses on the once thriving Jewish community in medieval Lecce.

Piazza del Duomo

Lecce's stunning **Piazza del Duomo**, west of Piazza Sant'Otranzo, is a triumph of Lecce Baroque, at its most theatrical at night when floodlit. This has always been a stage set for lavish religious and civic celebrations and today is the setting in summer for concerts and ballets. The piazza is framed by the facades of the Duomo, the Palazzo Vescovile (Episcopal Palace) and the Seminario (Seminary), all built or reworked in the seventeenth century. Unusually the **Duomo** has two facades: the theatrical one facing the opening to the piazza, conceived as a triumphal arch, and the more austere, older facade at the eastern end. The lofty campanile, built separately from the Duomo, formerly served as a watchtower. Today there is no public access – unless you are Madonna, who was allowed to climb to the top in 2017. Inside the Duomo, the riot of multi-coloured marble, gilt stucco and statues is typical of the ornate local style.

Overlooking the Piazzetta Vittorio Emanuele II, east of the Duomo, the **Chiesa di Santa Chiara** has a highly decorative facade and ornate altar as well as some remarkable examples of papier-mâché (*cartapesta*). Look up at the ceiling – you would never know it wasn't wood. The art dates back to the seventeenth century and most of the Lecce churches feature at least one *cartapesta* statue. There are still workshops in the city where you can buy finely crafted pieces.

Zimbalo is buried in the **Basilica di San Giovanni Battista** otherwise known as the **Basilica del Rosario** (Via Giuseppe Libertini

---

MUSEO ARCHEOLOGICO FAGGIANO

In 2001 Luciano Faggiano purchased a building on Via Ascanio Grandi in Lecce with the intention of creating a trattoria. The toilet was malfunctioning so he and his two elder sons dug down to find a sewage pipe. On the way they discovered two thousand years of history. Archeological finds on various levels of the foundations included a Messapian tomb, a Roman granary, etchings from the Knights Templar and remains from a Franciscan Convent. The trattoria was never built, digging went on for years and the building became a museum in 2008: the **Museo Archeologico Faggiano** (www.museofaggiano.it; charge). Around four thousand archeological artefacts were discovered, many of which are stored under Lecce's castle, others in the museum.

5; free). The exuberant facade is only rivalled by that of Lecce's Santa Croce.

Abbazia di Santa Maria di Cerrate

In a country setting amongst olive groves, 20 minutes' drive north of Lecce, lies the lovely Romanesque **Abbazia di Santa Maria di Cerrate** (www.fondoambiente.it/abbazia-di-santa-maria-di-cerrate-eng; free). This ex-Greek Orthodox monastery was once a cultural hub of southern Italy which later expanded into farming. The site was sacked by Turkish pirates in 1711 and left abandoned. In 2012 it was entrusted to the FAI, (Fondo Ambiente Italiano), the Italian National Trust, for major restoration and has recently opened to the public.

The mosaic floor inside Otranto Cathedral

The Grecia Salentina

South of Lecce lies the area known as Grecia Salentina, an area of Greek colonisation where you can still very occasionally hear the older generation speak *griko*, a Greek dialect. The first settlers arrived in the eighth century, fleeing from religious persecution in Greece. They founded monasteries, set up communities and began the wine and olive oil industries. By the tenth century there were around forty villages whose language,

OLIVE TREES IN PERIL

Puglia is renowned for olive trees, some of them centuries old. Until recently it produced around 40 percent of the olive oil exported from Italy. But in 2013 Salento was hit by a vicious bacterium, *Xyella fastidiosa*, believed to have arrived in Italy on exotic plants from Costa Rica. The cause is a tiny pest called the spittlebug. The result has been the desiccation of olive groves and the loss or threatened loss of business to families who have been producing olive oil for generations. Around a third of Puglia's olive trees have been affected and the disease is advancing north. In an effort to eradicate the spread an EU commission stipulated that farmers uproot infected trees and in some cases destroy other olive trees, however healthy, within 100m (109 yards) of the ones affected. There is no known cure but the felling of so many trees is hotly disputed, not just by farmers but by bacteria experts and plant pathologists who believe that the bacterium can be treated with natural remedies. Meanwhile the race is on to discover olive cultivars resistant to the disease which could replace the dead trees.

clothing, food and habits were entirely Greek. The Norman invasion in the early eleventh century saw the start of the decline of the villages, but there are still religious buildings dating from its Greek heyday, flat houses which look more Greek than Italian and signs in Greek as well as Italian. One of the remaining ten or so Greek villages is **Calimera** (Kalimera in Greek means 'good morning'), another is **Corigliano d'Otranto** ❷⁹ a former centre of Greek language and culture, with a dominant castle and a market where you might just catch a phrase or two of *griko*.

The Grecia Salentina hosts one of Europe's most important music festivals, dedicated to traditional culture: **La Notte della Taranta** (www.lanottedellataranta.it/en). The festival is dedicated to the rediscovery of Salento's folk music and its fusion with other genres of music, be it rock, jazz or classical. Every August over 200,000 spectators flock to the region to hear concerts in the villages, the grand finale being the famous Concertone, held at Melpignano. Each year the *taranta* folk dance is performed at the Festival of SS Pietro e Paolo (June 28–30) in the eponymous church at the town of **Galatina** ③⓪ on the edge of the Grecia Salentina. The main monument of this quite smart, ex-Greek city is the beautiful late Romanesque Basilica of Santa Caterina d'Alessandria whose walls are embellished with remarkable fourteenth-century frescoes depicting biblical scenes.

Otranto

South-east of Lecce, **Otranto** ③① is Italy's most easterly town, built on a rocky promontory and facing the shores of Albania. A town

Baia dei Turchi, popular for a reason

of Greek origin, it became the main port on the eastern coast of the Adriatic. The location made it vulnerable to attacks, the most notorious of which was the 1480 siege by an Ottoman fleet carrying eighteen thousand troops. The Otranto people refused to surrender. Thousands were killed, including all males over 15, and five thousand were enslaved. Some eight hundred survivors were offered mercy if they embraced the Muslim faith. They refused and were all beheaded, along with their executioner who was so impressed by their steadfastness that he announced an untimely conversion to the Christian faith. The Chiesa dei Martiri (Church of the Martyrs) on the Hill of Minerva just up from the centre, marks the spot where the eight hundred were beheaded. They were canonised by Pope Francis in 2013 and are known as the Blessed Martyrs of Otranto.

> **NOTES**
>
> Just over 10km (6 miles) south of Otranto lies a delightful secluded bay called Porto Badisco. Virgil cites it as the spot where Aeneas first stepped foot onto Italian shores after his escape from Troy. The crystalline waters are perfect for swimming, snorkelling and diving. In the rocks just to the north lies the Grotta dei Cervi (Cave of the Deer) with traces of prehistoric cave paintings including depictions of deer.

Castello and Cattedrale

Otranto's picturesque historic quarter, seafront restaurants and fine white beaches combine to make it one of Puglia's most sought-after resorts. (Steer clear in high season when it's teeming.) The old centre, on a hill, is heralded by the **Castello Aragonese** (https://cultura.gov.it/luogo/castello-di-otranto; charge), built by Ferdinand of Aragon in the late fifteenth century, following the Ottoman invasion of 1480. Many English who visit Otranto associate the town with Horace Walpole who wrote the novel *The Castle*

Santa Maria di Leuca

of Otranto (1764), generally regarded as the first Gothic novel. In fact the only reason he chose the title was because he liked the 'sonorous name' – he never actually went there.

But Otranto's star sight is the **Cattedrale dell'Annunziata** on Piazza Duomo, built by the Normans in the eleventh century. This church retains a stunning rose window and an even more stunning mosaic, covering the entire floor of the basilica. It represents *The Tree of Life*, whose branches bear naive depictions of the Labours of the Month (showing the relevant agricultural or domestic activity) and scenes from the Bible and mythology. In the right isle of the church the gruesome **Cappella dei Martiri** displays behind glass panels the bones of the martyrs slain by the Saracens. Otranto's first cathedral was the **Basilica di San Pietro** on Via San Pietro, in the oldest part of the town, a jewel of a church dating back to the ninth century with a Greek-cross plan and faded frescoes.

Otranto has long stretches of sandy beaches to the north of the town, backed by pine forests and lapped by the limpid, blue-green sea. One of the most sought-after beaches is the **Baia dei Turchi** ㉜, packed in high season when it is linked to Otranto by shuttle bus.

South from Otranto

Once you have reached Otranto it is hard to resist the temptation to visit Italy's Land's End at Santa Maria di Leuca. A wild and rocky shoreline, characterised by spits of land jutting into the sparkling seas and ruined watchtowers, gives way to a dramatic corniche running through small resorts. On a clear day, if you strain your

THE GREAT APULIAN AQUEDUCT

Man-made aqueducts in parched areas of Europe have existed since the sixth century BC when the ancient Greeks constructed the Eupalinian Aqueduct to supply Samos. But few people have heard of the 'The Great Aqueduct of Apulia', one of the most impressive hydraulic engineering systems in the world for size and capacity. Until World War I Puglia was seriously arid, bedevilled by poor farming conditions and poverty. There were no useful rivers to channel, so in the early twentieth century civil engineers tapped the water from the Sele River in the mountains in Campania on the western slope of the Apennine watershed. The first section, bringing water to Bari, was functioning by 1915 and the entire aqueduct was inaugurated in 1939 under Mussolini as part of his ambitious building programme. Today it stretches for 2,189km (1,360 miles), terminating at Santa Maria di Leuca, and serves four million Pugliesi in 258 cities, towns and villages. The solution of such a fundamental natural problem afflicting such a large region by a single engineering feat makes this aqueduct notable if not unique.

eyes, you might just spot the coast of Corfu and southern Albania. The drive is not recommended in high season when traffic can be nose-to-tail.

Castro

Roughly half way between Otranto and Santa Maria de Leuca is the appealing town of **Castro** ㉝, overlooking the sea. It dates back to pre-Roman times, has a fine Aragonese castle, built on foundations of earlier fortresses, a charming old town with a Romanesque cathedral and a rocky coast riddled with caves. Spectacular sea views can be enjoyed from the panoramic piazza above the port. The most famous of its caves is the seductively named **La Grotta Zinzulusa** ㉞

Gallipoli harbour and castle

(http://grottazinzulusacastro.it/; charge, guided tours only, accessible by boat and road), named after the stalactites that resemble dangling strips of cloth ('*zinzuli*' in local dialect). This is a highly popular tourist attraction although the caves are not as beautiful as those of Castellana (see page 60).

> **NOTES**
>
> In the sixteenth and seventeenth centuries Gallipoli was a prosperous city, exporting its renowned olive oil to many European capitals. This famous nectar was not used for drizzling on bread or salad but as fuel for the lamps in the city streets.

Santa Maria di Leuca

The resort town of **Santa Maria di Leuca** � lies at the end of the road, on the southern tip of Italy, where the Ionian and Adriatic seas meet. A sign in the piazza informs you that this is *Finibus Terrae*, the end of the earth as the Romans called it. Near the lighthouse on the windswept rocky promontory a column erected by Mussolini marks the terminus of the Apulian Aqueduct (see box). On the rare occasions when there is an excess of water the floodgates are opened, creating a monumental cascade of water into the sea. At the top of the hill near the lighthouse and overlooking the sea, the **Basilica Santuario di Santa Maria de Finibus Terrae** (www.basilicaleuca.it; free) is a place of pilgrimage constructed over the ruins of a pagan temple to Minerva and rebuilt many times after attacks by Moorish corsairs.

Gallipoli

Watchtowers dot the Ionian coastline between Santa Maria di Leuca and Gallipoli, with resorts and beaches in between. The 8km (5 mile) stretch of fine white sands and shallow crystalline water at **Marina di Pescoluse**, at the southern end, is known as the Maldives of Salento.

The historic port of **Gallipoli** ⓐ may not quite live up to its name (*Kalos Polis* means 'beautiful city' in Greek) but it certainly has plenty of charm and is well worth visiting for the old walled town, fishing port, churches, nearby beaches and delicious seafood dishes. The historic centre is set on an island which is joined to the new town by a bridge (in summer you have to park on the mainland and walk across). The prominent **Castello Angioino** (www.castellodigallipoli.it; charge) heralding the historic centre, was built by the Aragonese and remodelled in the seventeenth century. Today it is a cultural centre, hosting temporary exhibitions and concerts. Below the bridge, the **fish market** is one of the liveliest in Puglia, with a huge range of fish and seafood. Come for *Aperfish*, an early evening fish snack with an *aperitivo* and look out for *gamberoni viola* (purple prawns) *di Gallipoli*, a local speciality. The centre of the old town has handsome Spanish-style *palazzi* with courtyards, carvings and wrought-iron balconies. On one of the narrow cobbled alleyways is the Baroque **Cattedrale di Sant'Agata**, with its rich, honey-coloured facade. Nearby, the **Frantoio Ipogeo** is one of many underground tufa caves where olive oil used to be pressed – the city was a major exporter of olive oil in its heyday. A stroll around the **bastions** affords fine sea views, tavernas with terraces and some delightful Baroque churches to admire.

Taranto's Doric Columns

THE TARANTELLA OR PIZZICA

If you are lucky enough to coincide with one of Puglia's festivals you may well hear the hypnotic music of the *taranta*, named after Taranto. Folklore has it that in the fifteenth to seventeenth centuries women working in the fields were bitten by Lycosa tarantula spiders (not to be confused with what is commonly known as a tarantula today) and infected with 'tarantism', the only cure for which was believed to be a frenzied non-stop spinning dance. This became known as the *tarantella* (also locally known as 'pizzica', which means bite, sting or pinch, referring to the spider's bite). There is no evidence that these spider bites were poisonous, but the story has been passed down through the generations. Today's tarantella is not the hysterical dance of yore and is nearly always performed by two women or a man and a woman. It is most commonly accompanied by a mandolin, guitar, accordion and tambourine and varies from region to region. The main *taranta* event in Puglia is the Notte della Taranta, which tours around Salento and culminates in Melpignano in August.

Taranto

Founded by Spartan colonisers in 706 BC, ancient **Taras (Taranto)** ❸⓻ was in the fourth century BC the largest city in Magna Graecia, boasting a population of 300,000 and a city wall 15km (9 miles) in circumference. It became a thriving commercial seaport, a hub of art and culture and, like many communities throughout Magna Graecia, a centre of Pythagorean philosophy. All that remains of this era in Taranto are two columns of what was one of the most important Doric temples in Magna Graecia, dedicated to the god Poseidon.

The steelworks and huge cranes as you approach Taranto don't endear you to the city and the old town on a small island is notoriously dark, dingy and run-down (watch your valuables and avoid going off the beaten track). In comparison the new eighteenth- and nineteenth-century town, on the mainland, is quite elegant and is visited by sightseers for the city's outstanding archeological museum.

MArTA (Museo Archeologico Nazionale di Taranto)

Most tourists give Taranto a wide berth but for anyone interested in ancient Taras it is worth a visit if only for the **MArTA** or **Museo Archeologico Nazionale di Taranto** (Via Cavour 10; www.museotaranto.beniculturali.it; charge). In southern Italy it is rivalled only by Naples' Archeological Museum for the splendour of its antiquities. Archeological finds and artefacts, numbering around 200,000, range from the Paleolithic era through to the early Middle Ages. The exhibits include Greek and Roman sculpture, a series of

Grottaglie, famous for its ceramics since medieval times

wonderful Roman floor mosaics, one of the most important collections of ancient ceramics in Italy and, perhaps most famous of all, a collection of gold artefacts including exquisite jewellery from Magna Graecia.

Old town

The *centro storico* or old town, bounded by the Small and the Great Seas, and accessed over the Ponte Girevole from the mainland, is dominated by the splendid **Castello Aragonese** (www.castelloaragonesetaranto.com; free). The castle, with its four sturdy cylindrical towers, was built in the fifteenth century to defend the city against invading Turks. In the eighteenth century it was converted into a prison, then donated in 1887 to the Italian Navy who still occupy it and Italian officers in uniform will show you round. Opposite the castle is the Baroque **Palazzo di Città**, palace of the governor (closed to the public).

Across the square from the castle are the two remaining **Doric Columns** from the Greek Temple. A stroll along the waterfront will bring you to the cloistered **Convento Santa Chiara** and, turning right up Vico Santa Chiara, to the **Cattedrale di San Cataldo**. This was redesigned in Baroque style in the seventeenth and eighteenth century, and is notable for the inlaid marble and frescoes in the **Cappellone di San Cataldo**. This chapel houses relics of Taranto's patron saint, San Cataldo, who was to become its archbishop. Via Duomo leads to the **Chiesa di San Domenico**, founded by Frederick II in 1223, and today showcases a blend of medieval and Baroque.

The workshops of Grottaglie

East of Taranto, on a small hill, the town of **Grottaglie** ⓴ takes its name from the grottoes carved from the *tufo*. Artisans here have been producing hand-made ceramics since medieval times. There are around 50 workshops, many of them sited within the caves. Head for the *quartiere delle ceramiche* (ceramics quarter) along Via E Crispi, to watch potters turning clay, painting and creating jugs, urns, pots, crockery, lamps and decorative figures. Prices and quality vary but it is not hard to find beautifully made pieces in colourful traditional designs. Avoid afternoons when the workshops are closed and note that on Sundays only some are open. The Museo della Ceramica (http://cultura.gov.it/luogo/museo-della-ceramica-di-grottaglie; charge), displaying four hundred pieces, charts the history of the local ceramics industry from the fourteenth to the twentieth century.

An excursion to Matera

Highlights
- **'City of Shame'**, see page 88
- **Seeing the city**, see page 90
- **The Sassi**, see page 91
- **The new town**, see page 93
- **Parco della Murgia Materana**, see page 93

The city of **Matera** ❸❾ is located in the region of Basilicata rather than Puglia but it is only just across the border and it's well worth adding an extra day or two to your stay in Puglia to explore this intriguing city. It is just under 70km (43 miles) from Bari. The journey takes 65 minutes by bus (or 75 minutes by shuttle bus from the airport), 1hr 45 minutes by train and 60–70 minutes by car. Parking is prohibited in the old city (though you can usually drop your luggage if you're staying overnight) and finding a parking place in the new town is notoriously difficult.

'City of Shame'
Designated a UNESCO World Heritage Site in 1993 and the first southern Italian city to be recognised as European Capital of Culture (2019), this is a beguiling town of troglodyte dwellings,

Beguiling Matera

evocative cave churches, houses piled on top of each other and abandoned hovels – all gouged out of the limestone *tufo* over the ages. It is said to be the third oldest continuously inhabited city in the world, with some caves dating back to the Palaeolithic age. Up until the 1950s the honeycomb of houses and caves known as Sassi (rocks) were home to peasants who lived in appalling conditions with an average of six children, together with the animals, in a single room. The Italian government, embarrassed by the 'City of Shame', moved out (at times forcefully) fifteen thousand residents into new, more modern quarters from 1953–68. In the 1980s a number of intrepid Materani started to return. Now the Sassi are Basilicata's main tourist attraction, recognised by UNESCO as 'the most outstanding, intact example of a troglodyte settlement in the Mediterranean region'.

CHRIST STOPPED AT EBOLI

Carlo Levi, the Italian writer, painter and doctor, likened the Matera region to Dante's *Inferno* in his documentary novel: *Christ Stopped at Eboli* (1945). In 1935–36 Levi was exiled for his anti-Fascist activities to the remote village of Aliano (fictional name of Gagliano), 60km (37 miles) inland from Matera, where he wrote the novel. An account of his experience as a political prisoner and a study of the plight of the peasants which he witnessed in southern Italy, the novel was quickly acclaimed a literary masterpiece. In 1979 the book was adapted into a film. The Biblical landscapes around Matera have made perfect backdrops to several other films including Mel Gibson's *The Passion of The Christ* (2004), Pier Paolo Pasolini's *The Gospel According to St Matthew* (1964) and the James Bond film *No Time to Die* (2021).

Carlo Levi's sister, a doctor, had visited malaria-ridden Matera in 1936 and wrote of *'children with the faces of wizened old men, their bodies reduced by starvation almost to skeletons, their heads crawling with lice and covered with scabs'*. They were suffering from trachoma, malaria and dysentery.

Seeing the city

A ridge, crowned by Matera's cathedral, splits the Sassi into two: the Sasso Barisano and the Sasso Caveoso. Both are a labyrinth of alleys, stone stairways and tiny courtyards. The best way to explore them is on foot, stopping perhaps at bars or restaurants to see the clever conversions from the original cave dwellings. But even with a map, GPS or the brown itinerary signs it's easy to get lost in the warren of multilayered alleys. Many visitors opt for a guided tour (arranged by the tourist office or one of the agencies). These are usually good value, informative and give access to Sassi which are otherwise inaccessible. Alternatively the tourist office provides a map of Matera with suggested itineraries.

The more interesting church interiors are those of the so-called *chiese rupestri*: the primitive churches carved into the hillsides by monks in the ninth to the fifteenth centuries. There are around 150 of these churches, with some 48 in the *Sassi* themselves, some preserving remarkable frescoes which you can admire to the sounds of background music (anything from Gregorian chants to *The Sound of Silence*). Most churches are open daily from 10am–7pm, with shorter hours in the winter months. There is a charge for the rupestrian churches but cumulative tickets are available.

The Sassi

You could spend several days exploring all the churches but if time is limited concentrate on the following half dozen. In the **Sasso Barisano** the highlights are the **Chiesa San Pietro Barisano**, with

Chiesa Santa Maria de Idris

fifteenth- and sixteenth-century frescoes and burial niches where corpses were placed so that bodily fluids could drain into the porous rock, and the remarkable monastic complex of the **Chiesa di Madonna delle Virtù** and the **Chiesa di San Nicola dei Greci** above it, with glowing frescoes on the walls.

In the **Sasso Caveoso** it is worth seeking out the frescoed **Chiesa Santa Maria de Idris**, carved into the Idris rock and leading into the older and very evocative cave church of **San Giovanni in Monterrone**. The nearby basilica-style **Chiesa di Santa Lucia alle Malve** preserves some of its eleventh- to seventeenth-century frescoes, the most famous of which depicts a breastfeeding Madonna.

Inside a cave house in Matera

For an insight into bygone life you can visit caves which have been left more or less untouched since they were inhabited in the 1940s. Guides will tell you how cave-dwellers eked out a living, what they ate, how they washed and cooked and their ingenious systems to gather water from roofs, houses and streets. The **Casa-Grotta di Vico Solitario** in the Sasso Caveoso is set up as it would have been in the past, with a bed, a corner for pigs and chickens, an area for manure and straw, a trough for the mule and a terracotta chamber pot.

> **NOTES**
>
> Matera has some very atmospheric accommodation in converted caves and it's well worth seeing the city in the evening, when the crowds have gone and the buildings are bathed in a golden light.

The new town

In contrast to the Sassi is the **Piazza Vittorio Veneto,** the heart of the new town, a smart and spacious square overlooked by cafés, Baroque churches and elegant *palazzi*. In the evenings this is where you'll see the *passeggiata*. Below the piazza lies the **Palombaro Lungo**, a giant cistern which can be visited on guided tours. Dramatically located on a spur between the two Sassi the Romanesque-style **Cattedrale di Matera** (free) has a handsome golden-stone facade with a fine rose window. The interior was remodelled in elaborate Baroque style.

Parco della Murgia Materana

Across the gorge the **Parco della Murgia Materana** is home to abandoned caves and rock-cut churches – many of them created by monks fleeing from persecution. This is the site of some of the very oldest cave-dwellings. Although you can walk or drive there and leave the car at the top of the hill, it is tricky to reach some of the churches and you may want to join a guided tour. From here there are fabulous views of the Sassi across the gorge.

Cycling from Otranto to Leuca along the coast

Things to do

Culture

Puglia has a very lively musical scene. The folk sounds and dances of the **taranta** and **pizzica** are the soundtrack to many of the local celebrations, with the warm (and sometimes wild) participation of residents and visitors of all ages and from all walks of life. Attending a *sagra* or a *pizzica* night is highly recommended for all those who wish to better understand local culture.

When it comes to indie, electronic, pop and reggae **music**, Puglia has its own share of alternative and innovative bands and composers, many of whom have become famous beyond the regional borders.

Summer music festivals, whether classical or rock, often host big names in music. The **Itria Valley Festival** in Martina Franca (www.festivaldellavalleditria.it), lasting over a month in July, has a fabulous program of classical concerts and opera, performed 'under the stars'. The **Viva! Festival** (www.vivafestival.it) in Fasano and Locorotondo, happening in August, brings together music, nature and local culture, with concerts and performances by international stars. **FestAmbienteSud** in Vieste (end of July; www.festambientesud.it) explores environmental themes and also organizes great concerts that explore blends of musical and cultural influences. The **Night of the Taranta** (www.lanottedellataranta.it), taking place in Malpignano in late August, is the quintessential Puglian music festival. It is dedicated to the promotion of *taranta* worldwide, and broadcast on national television.

When it comes to highbrow entertainment, both Bari and Lecce enjoy a programme of ballet, opera and classical music.

In Bari, the most important theatre is the **Teatro Petruzzelli** (Corso Cavour 12; www.fondazionepetruzzelli.com), a resplendent theatre in the centre of town, staging local and international opera, ballet and concerts. Built in the early twentieth century it was destroyed by fire in 1991, then rebuilt in the same style and reopened in 2009 after years of criminal and civil law suits. It is the fourth largest theatre in Italy. Bari's oldest theatre is the **Teatro Piccinni** (1854) in Corso Vittorio Emanuele, named after Niccolò Piccinni, the eighteenth-century composer who hailed from Bari. The **Teatro Kursaal Santalucia**, a fine late Art Nouveau theatre, reopened in 2021 after a decade of closure to host cinema, theatre and cultural exhibitions.

Lecce's main theatre, the **Teatro Politeama Greco** (Via XXV Luglio 30; www.politeamagreco.it) hosts shows and concerts as well as plays. Every November Lecce hosts the **Festival del Cinema Europeo** (Festival of European Cinema) featuring the latest European releases.

Monument of Niccolò Piccinni

Nightlife

In recent years, the **Salento** has emerged as the most popular nightlife destination for the young, particularly in summer on the beaches. Hundreds of young people flock to Gallipoli from all over Italy for the cocktail bars, beach parties, clubs, open-air discos and non-stop dancing, starting in the afternoon. Other lively spots with beach nightlife (but not on the scale of Gallipoli) are **Porto Cesareo**, **Santa Maria di Leuca** and, on the Adriatic coast, **Santa**

Terme Cesarea and **Castro**. The Salento has a rich calendar of festivals and events, enlivening the squares and streets of city centres at night.

Although Puglia's nightlife is mainly concentrated on the coasts, the historic centres of Lecce and Bari, both of which are university cities, offer an excellent selection of restaurants and watering holes, from rustic little bars to trendy places with craft beers, exotic cocktails and live music. In Bari, Piazza Mercantile in the old city is one of the liveliest spots, with wine bars and restaurants lining the square

> **NOTES**
>
> One of the greatest forms of entertainment for Italians is the time-honoured *passeggiata* or ritual evening stroll. Families dress up and take to the main streets or piazzas to admire and be admired. Join the throng, preferably with a gelato in hand. In mid-summer the stroll goes on late into the night.

Outdoor activities

Puglia has increasing appeal for active visitors, offering year-round biking and hiking and plenty of scope for watersports enthusiasts and beach-lovers.

Cycling

Cycling is popular in Puglia but avoid July and August when the heat is intense, and the traffic (both cars and bikes along cycleways) is at its worst. The best time for a cycling holiday is spring or autumn. The most challenging and one of the most rewarding regions is the mountainous Gargano Peninsula. Further south it's easier cycling along the flat coastland and a gently undulating interior. Cycling is popular in and around the Itria Valley, also in the Salentine cities of Lecce, Gallipoli and Otranto. An increasing number of hotels have bikes for guest use, often with no charge.

Alternatively you can hire them in most towns and resorts and it's worth asking at tourist offices for cycle maps with recommended routes. For online maps of cycle paths and itineraries go to www.pisteciclabili.com and click on Apulia.

Several companies specialise in **cycling holidays**, both self-guided and guided, from half a day to a week or more. Self-guided tours typically include accommodation with breakfast, luggage transport, GPS devices programmed with routes, tracks, detailed maps, route notes, 24-hour assistance and medical and luggage insurance; guided tours, some of which are e-bike tours, will include dinners and probably local food tastings en route.

The following offer **biking tours** throughout Puglia: 4Cycling 'n Trek (www.4cyclingandtrek.com), Ciclovagando (www.ciclovagando.com) and Puglia Cycle tours (www.pugliacycletours.com).

Adriatic Cycle Route

The Ciclovia Adriatica (Adriatic Cycle Route) is a national tourist cycle route of about 1300km (808 miles) linking Trieste with Santa Maria di Leuca, Puglia's southernmost tip. The Apulian section extends over 500km (311 miles). South of the Gargano Peninsula the route runs for the most part through flat terrain at sea level and takes you mainly on secondary, rural roads with little traffic.

Hiking

Puglia has **hiking trails** throughout the region, from the forests of the mountainous Gargano Peninsula to the ancient shepherds' paths and along the rugged coast of Salento. The best time to go is spring or autumn. A popular region for a week's walking is the gently undulating Valle d'Itria, through peaceful olives groves and vineyards, and staying overnight at the characteristic hilltop 'white cities'. Macs Adventure (www.macsadventure.com) organise self-guided short breaks or easy to moderate 64km (40 miles)

Diving off the Tremiti Islands

one-week walking tours, starting in Alberobello and ending at Otranto, with transfers, train journey from Ostuni to Lecce and accommodation (with one night in a *trullo*) all included in the deal.

Watersports

The crystalline waters make for excellent **snorkelling** and **diving**, with caves, shipwrecks and rich flora and fauna adding to the attraction. Among the best areas are the Tremiti Islands and Salento. Scuba diving centres can be found at many of the main resorts and typically offer programmes for complete beginners to dive-master level. The Tremiti Diving Center (www.tremitidivingcenter.com) on the Tremiti Islands offers a full day snorkelling as well as scuba courses. At Santa Maria di Leuca on the southern tip of Italy you can dive down to the statue of the

Lady of the Two Seas, seeing octopuses, nudibranchs and sometimes even seahorses as you go. A deeper dive takes you down to the Torre Vado wreck, a Turkish merchant ship on the seabed or for more experienced divers there are 50m (164ft) dives into the open sea, with shoals of barracuda and large groupers (Salento Diving, www.salentodiving.it).

With its medium to strong winds and large sandy beaches Salento is the best place for **kitesurfing** and **windsurfing**. Schools offer courses for all levels of windsurfing but waves and choppy seas at some beaches are not suitable for beginners. The main spots on the Adriatic are Frassanito and San Foca, and on the Ionian coast Gallipoli, Porto Cesareo, Torre Mozza and Torre San Giovanni.

Poolside at Vair Spa

Beaches and boat trips

Puglia has 800km (500 miles) of coastline, glorious blue seas and some superlative beaches. But it is by no means all pristine white sands and Riviera-like resorts. Much of the coast is dry, rocky terrain and some of it is lined by unsightly development and dirty beaches. The best of the beaches are those on the Gargano Peninsula and in Salento. Try and avoid the second half of July and the whole of August when the sands are packed with

Italian holidaymakers. Some beaches charge a fee for access. In Salento there are some exclusive beach clubs with upmarket facilities and prices to match (a couple of sunbeds with a parasol close to the sea in July or August could set you back €80 and parking may well add another €10; in 2023 the beach of Pescoluse made the news for being the most expensive beach in Italy).

Many resorts offer boat or yacht excursions to explore coastal grottoes, striking rock formations or even dolphin-spotting. Alternatively you can rent a jet-ski, dinghy or motorboat and explore independently.

Other activities

Horseriding is a great way to discover the local landscape. The A.S.D. Centro Equestre Parco di Mare equestrian sea park at Montalbano di Fasano, 14km (8.5 miles) east of Fasano (www.parcodimare.com) is a long-established equestrian centre with classes for all levels and excursions to the countryside and coast. In Salento the Centro Equitazione Altosalento (www.equitazionealtosalento.it/en) offers courses from show jumping and dressage to pony games for children. Many of the *masserie* (converted farmhouses) offer horseriding.

Golf is not big here but Puglia has a handful of courses, the best of which is the San Domenico Golf at Savelletri di Fasano (www.sandomenicogolf.com), 66km (41 miles) southeast of Bari. This is a challenging 18-hole course with fine views of the Adriatic. San Domenico Golf owns the luxury *Masseria San Domenico* and offers substantial discounts on green fees to guests.

Spas

In the land of olives, almonds and vineyards you can indulge in spa treatments with olive oil, almond oil and red wine. If money is no object opt for a dose of pampering at the award-winning Vair Spa at the luxury *Borgo Egnazia* (www.borgoegnazia.com). This is a soothing, exclusive, candlelit sanctuary, with personalised consultations and treatments to revitalise mind, body and spirit. The team includes barefoot therapists in trailing robes, nutritionists, artists, musicians and dancers.

The main spa town is Santa Cesarea Terme in Salento, 35km (21 miles) south of Lecce. The springs of sulphurous water, which flow from four caves along the coast, have made it an important thermal centre for specialised medical cures and personalized treatments.

Shopping

A region renowned for olive oil, pasta and wine, Puglia is packed with little shops and delis selling gastronomic delights.

Where to shop

Most towns have a market once a week, selling fresh fruit, vegetables, seafood, meat and typical Puglian specialities. Markets typically open at 8am and are more or less finished by lunchtime so make an early start. Most town centres are filled with small shops and boutiques that make for a very pleasant shopping experience. *Agriturismi* and *masserie* sometimes have their own shops selling their olive oil and preserves, but if you are looking for delicious local foods to bring back it may sometimes even be enough to just visit a local supermarket like Conad for great pastas, cheeses and cured meats.

What to buy

Pasta. The local pasta is *orecchiette*, 'little ears'. You can see it being made by hand in the backstreets of Bari's old town and you can learn how to make it from scratch at local cooking classes. Shops all over Puglia sell packets of dried *orecchiette*.

Salumi and cheese. *Salumerie* (delicatessens) offer a tempting range of cured meats and cheeses. In Bari the Antica Salumeria del Gusto, at Piazza Nicola Balenzano 12/A, is a long-established family-run *salumeria* and something of a Bari institution, offering a feast of Puglian cheeses, including ricotta, burrata and *stracciatella* as well as cured meats, olive oils and wines. It is hard to resist an impromptu lunch at the counter. Il Salumaio, at Via Piccinni 168 is another one of Bari's wonderful delis to explore.

Taralli. *Taralli,* or small rings, similar in texture to a breadstick or pretzel, are sold all over Puglia. In Lecce's Golosità del Salento dal 1942, at Via A.Petronelli 3, you can find a whole variety from fennel, black olive or poppy-seed flavours to sweet *taralli* which can be dunked in wine. This is an enticing shop, with other specialities such as variously flavoured extra virgin olive oils, almond-stuffed figs, turnip-top pesto and multicoloured *orecchiette*.

Olive oil. Puglia produces around 40 percent of Italy's olive oil. It's known for its extra virgin olive oil or 'the green gold of Puglia' and is used in beauty products such as body creams, shampoos and sun lotions as well as for culinary use. Fans can follow the Strada dell'Olio di Puglia (Puglia's Olive Oil Road) extending for 140km (87 miles) in the province of Brindisi, with plenty of opportunities to taste and buy. Bottles or tins of Puglia's oil can be found wherever you go and sometimes there are stalls by the roadside. The main extra virgin Puglia olive oil DOP

Making orecchiette in Bari

producers are Collina di Brindisi, Dauno DOP in the Foggia region and Terra d'Otranto DOP in Salento.

Wine. The full-bodied red Primitivo and Negroamaro are the stars of the region (see page 114), available from *enotecas* (wine shops/bars) as well as most food shops.

Papier-mâché (*cartapesta*). Dozens of papier-mâché sculptures decorate churches but they look so like wood, marble or stone, it's impossible to tell the difference. Lecce is the main centre with several *cartapesta* workshops in the old town selling finely handcrafted statues and figurines. *Cartapesta* dates back to the seventeenth century when it was used as a cheaper alternative to traditional materials. To learn the craft, join a *cartapesta* class at Laboratorio Cartapesta Riso, Via Vittorio Emanuele II 27, Lecce.

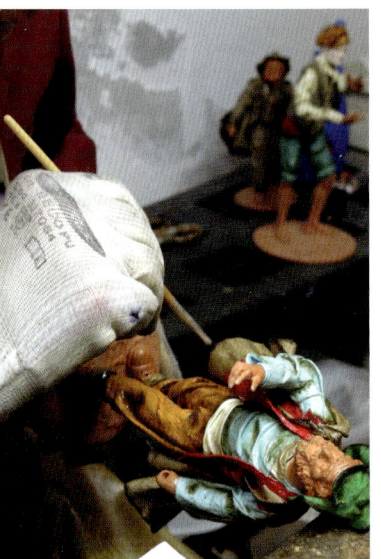

Cartapesta artisan at work in Lecce

Linen. In the centre of Lecce, Society, at Via degli Ammirati 6 (www.epiphanysociety.com), sells fine and stylish household linen. Despite the name, this is an Italian brand which creates beautiful tablecloths, stunning bed linen, comfy bathrobes and quality napkins and scarves, which come in a wide range of colours for you to choose from.

Ceramics and pottery. The ceramics' capital of southern Italy is the town of Grottaglie, 23km (14 miles) east of Taranto. The ceramics quarter has around fifty workshops, where you can watch the potters at work and choose from pots, vases, tiles, lamps, crockery and ornaments. Avoid afternoons, when the workshops are shut, and Sundays, when less than half are open. The tradition goes back to medieval times and some of the ceramicists still use traditional techniques and designs. The Fasanos at Fasano Ceramiche (Via Francesco Crispi 6) have been creating ceramics since the nineteenth century and the family tradition carries on today with shops in Milan and Rome as well as Grottaglie. Purchases can be shipped home.

> **NOTES**
>
> Note that shops abide by the local custom of *siesta*, closing their doors from around 1pm–4.30/5.30pm, then staying open until around 7.30/8pm.

Fashion. Bari is the best bet for fashion and its Via Sparano is the place to go for big names in designer boutiques. The Puglia Village outlet at Molfetta (https://pugliavillage.it/en/home) 33km (20.5 miles) northwest of Bari, has over 140 boutiques and shops selling designer fashions, accessories, cosmetics and sports equipment. Molfetta can be reached from Bari by train and a shuttle bus service links its station with the outlet.

Children

The Italians adore children and the Pugliesi are no exception. Although there are few attractions specifically designed for youngsters, the island offers sandy, gently shelving beaches, many of them Blue Flag. However, seas can be quite rough and parents should take heed of the warning flags. The small rocky coves are fun for children to explore and older ones who are strong swimmers can enjoy jumping off the rocks into the sea. Polignano al Mare is famous for the Red Bull Cliff Diving contest (see page 57) and has lower rocks for children to jump off. A day's excursion to the Tremiti Islands (see

La Notte della Taranta in Melpignano

page 40) is likely to appeal with boat trips to caves and grottoes, and snorkelling in crystalline waters. Older children will enjoy exploring all the castles. For accommodation you can stay in the hobbit-style *trulli* or *agriturismi* (holiday farms) where children can enjoy outdoor pursuits such as cherry-picking or exploring the countryside on horseback, bike or foot.

The main attraction in Puglia aimed specifically at children is Zoo Safari (Via dello Zoosafari, close to Fasano; www.zoosafari.it). This is a large animal theme park with a drive-through, safari-style park (taking your own car) where giraffes block your way or peer through the car windows. Be prepared for long queues in summer. Neighbouring Fasanolandia is a theme park under the same management, with amusement rides and water slides. The other big hit with children (though not tiny ones) are the spectacular caves of Grotte di Castellana (see page 60).

Festivals and events

This is just a handful of the hundreds of events in Puglia throughout the year. Ask at the local tourist office to find out what's on.

January–April Il Carnevale di Putignano, one of Europe's oldest carnivals, with various events up to Shrove Tuesday including four parades, parties and mocking masquerades. Some events also take place in summer. A mini summer carnival also takes place in early July.

March–April Easter week with processions and passion plays throughout Puglia.

Late April Bari International Film Festival (one week).

May 7–9 Bari celebrates the three-day Festa di San Nicola, when thousands of pilgrims from all over the world descend on the city.

May 8–10 La Festa di San Cataldo held in Taranto. Three days of celebration, honouring the city's patron saint.

End of June Danza delle Tarantole (Dance of the Tarantella) at Galatina.

July Fasano Music Festival. Otranto three-day Jazz Festival at the castle; La Ghironda, Ostuni festival.

Mid-July for two months Bari in Jazz Festival, in the capital and other towns.

Mid-July to early Aug Festival della Valle d'Itria at Martina Franca: classical music festival, including opera.

August 2–3 weeks La Notte della Taranta in Melpignano is the largest of several events across Salento, celebrating the tarantella dance. Concerts, bands, dancing, folk-music.

Mid-August Festival of the Holy Martyrs in Otranto commemorates the 1480 massacre of eight hundred residents by Turkish forces.

August 23 Festa di Sant'Oronzo in Lecce, dedicated to the town's patron saint. Musical events, food stalls and fireworks. Fish festival in Polignano a Mare.

Late September Commemorations in San Giovanni Rotondo on the anniversary of the passing of Padre Pio (1968). Monte Sant'Angelo festival.

October Sagra ti li stacchioddi in Latiano, celebrating *orecchiette* in their many variations.

November Lecce hosts the European Film Festival (six days).

December Christmas festivities, religious events and nativity scenes.

Food and drink

Eating out is one of the great pleasures of a holiday in Puglia. What's more, provided you don't tuck into too many *pasticciotti* (egg-custard pies), it's a healthy diet, based on vegetables, fruit, extra virgin olive oil, pasta made with durum flour (high in protein and melatonin) and fish fresh from the sea. The vast plains of Puglia produce abundant fruit, vegetables and wheat, the sixty or so million olive trees yield 40 percent of Italy's olive oil exports and the vines produce 17 percent of Italy's total wine production.

The local cuisine is the deeply-rooted *cucina povera*, the so-called 'poor cuisine', though nowadays it's a fashionable renaissance of cheap and abundant staples, in some cases served in trendy settings and prepared with a creative touch. The best known dishes, such as (eggless) pasta with chickpeas, broad bean purée with wild chicory or mussels baked with potato and rice, are based on the humblest ingredients. Seasonality and freshness of ingredients are key, and generally there's increased attention to the needs of vegetarian, vegan or gluten-free visitors, especially in the bigger towns.

SAGRE: IMMERSIVE CULTURAL EXPERIENCES

A great way to immerse yourself in local culture and enjoy Puglia's culinary delights is to head to a *sagra*. Happening all year round, usually in the evening, *sagre* are lively local festivals that celebrate a new crop, a particular food or a dish, sometimes in combination with a religious or pagan holiday, a boat race or a historic commemoration. *Sagre* are not just about the food; they also feature live music, dancing and market stalls in a lively atmosphere. The almond festival in Specchia, the fritter festival of Latiano and the octopus festival in Mola di Bari, all happening in July, are some of the popular ones, but head to the local tourist office for up-to-date information.

Ricci di mare

In a region with 800km (500 miles) of coastline, fish and seafood obviously play a major role in the local cuisine and on most menus fish will predominate over meat.

Where to eat

Main meals are served in a *ristorante*, *trattoria* or *osteria* but the difference between the three is negligible these days. An *osteria*, traditionally a tavern or inn serving wine and pasta, can nowadays range from traditional to hip. A pizzeria often extends to pasta and meat dishes and the better ones serve pizza bubbling hot from a wood-fired brick oven. The Italians prefer to eat pizza in the evening and to accompany it with beer rather than wine. *Pizza al taglio*, sold by the slice, is a popular takeaway. For a quick bite go to a bar or café where you can find a selection of rolls and sandwiches.

Enjoy snacking on taralli

Standing at the bar (*al banco*) is usually cheaper than sitting at a table with waiter service, especially in the more touristy areas. An *enoteca* or wine bar will have a serious selection of wines, many available by the glass, and an optional platter of cheese or cold meats to accompany them. Many *masserie* and *agriturismi* will have their own restaurant serving local specialities. These too can range from simple and rural to luxurious and trendy. For a deep dive into local flavours and culture, visit a *sagra* (see page 108). For those in search of a more refined food experience, there's a whole new wave of food and wine festivals that have emerged in recent years. Showcasing the excellence of local produce and culinary tradition, these festivals also include demonstrations by chefs, tasting events and workshops. A good example is the EGO Festival in Taranto, in May (www.egofestival.it).

A Puglian meal: the basics

As in the rest of Italy, restaurants offer four courses: *antipasti* (starters), the *primo* (first course, typically pasta but also risotto or soup), the *secondo* (main course of fish or meat) and the *dolce* (dessert), followed perhaps by cheese, an *espresso* and a *digestivo*. Not that you would be expected, these days, to wade through every course. Set menus vary from a basic two or three-course meal, usually with a choice of meat or fish, to a seven-course blow-out *menu degustazione* giving you the chance to try several house specialities. All set menus include service and cover charge; some also throw in house wine, mineral water and coffee. Some of the smaller restaurants don't have menus at all and may bring out seemingly never-ending courses without telling you what they are going to be. This is where a few words of Italian could be very useful.

Antipasti

Antipasti, or starters, are often the highlight of the meal, enabling you to sample several of the local specialities. Most menus offer an impressive array including seafood, *salumi* (cold cuts), cheeses and vegetables.

Il primo

Most of Puglia's pasta is made from just flour and water, a tradition which goes back to the time when eggs were beyond the pockets of the Pugliesi. The pasta is nicely chewy and flavoursome and comes in all shapes and sizes. *Orecchiette* or 'little ears' are shaped to hold the sauce and this remains the region's signature pasta, most frequently cooked *con cime di rapa*. *Orecchiette* and other pastas come with *pomodori e ricotta forte* (tomatoes and double-fermented ricotta), *pomodori, cipolle e capocollo* (cherry tomatoes, red onions and diced *capocollo* – dried cured pork) or with *ragù di carne* (meat sauce). Seafood pastas are prevalent and often a delicious treat to try in the area of Puglia.

Il secondo

Along the coasts, fish fans are spoilt for choice. Main courses range from stuffed or skewered cuttlefish, grilled or steamed octopus to seabass, swordfish and tuna. Fish comes simply grilled, lightly fried or baked, often with a crust. *Fritto misto di mare* is mixed fried fish, normally including *calamari*, anchovies and prawns. In

Bari and elsewhere the Spaniards left their mark with *tiella*, a pie that resembles paella. In many restaurants smaller fish are served whole at a set price whereas the larger will be charged by the *etto* (100g). It's quite normal to ask to see the size of a portion first and check the price.

Menus are mainly fish-focussed but most will feature a handful of meat options. Traditional meats are chicken, lamb and kid but don't be surprised to see horse, donkey or slow-cooked offal on menus. Beef was a luxury in the past but with the advent of tourism steaks now often feature on menus. Martina Franca's speciality is *capocollo* (dry-cured pork, see page 63). Just to the east, the hilltop town of Cisternino is known for butchers-cum-tavernas where you queue up to choose your meat and have it roasted or grilled.

Vegetables and cheese

Puglia produces superb vegetables. A local favourite is the deliciously smooth chicory and broad bean purée, usually served as a starter and drizzled with extra virgin olive oil. Popular too is *parmigiana di melanzane* made with layers of sliced, fried aubergine, tomato sauce and cheese and baked in the oven. The most commonly found vegetables are *cime di rapa* (turnip greens), *fave* (broad beans), *ceci* (chickpeas, often preserved for the winter months), *cavolo* (cabbage) and *finocchio* (fennel) – as well as the antipasti vegetables (see page 111). When it comes to mushrooms pride of place goes to the huge *cardoncelli*, which grow near Bari in central Puglia. These are very versatile and are used in rich pasta sauces or stuffed with breadcrumbs, garlic and parsley, layered with potatoes and onions, sprinkled with breadcrumbs and baked in an earthenware dish.

Although it's not always easy to find restaurants that specialise in vegetarian or vegan fare, most can serve vegetable antipasti and a pasta with vegetables.

Puglia also has its fair share of local cheeses: *caciocavallo* is a pear-shaped cow's-milk cheese, named 'horse cheese' as it is traditionally hung to mature over a pole known as the *cavallo* ('horse'). More common is *mozzarella*, a traditional southern Italian cheese made from Italian buffalo's milk. *Burrata* is a deliciously creamy fresh cheese, made with buffalo or cow's milk. Make sure to look out too for aged, crumbly *pecorino* made from sheep's milk, which sometimes comes with peppercorns as well and is a delight to try.

Gelato and pastries

Pastries popular with Pugliesi, especially for breakfast, are *cornetti* (croissants) with custard cream or other fillings, and *pasticciotti*, little pies made with short-cut pastry and filled with ricotta or lemon custard. Gelaterie abound, offering all the usual flavours plus specialties such as almond (*mandorla*) ice cream and many sorbettos.

Drinks

Italian beer is excellent: ask for a *birra nazionale* and you will probably be served a bottle of Peroni. Recent years have seen a growth in the number of craft beers. Numerous bars and particularly cocktail bars serve an *aperitivo* with a complimentary selection of savouries.

Orecchiette

Pecorino from Vieste

Puglia yields around 15 percent of Italy's wine, producing spicy reds as well as a few whites.

Puglia's major wine district is Salento, and the three main grape varieties are all reds: Negroamaro, Primitivo and Malvasia Nera. Beware of the very high alcohol level – the minimum strength 14 percent but it can often be higher. Look out also for DOC Salice Salentino, produced primarily from the Negroamaro grape and named after the eponymous town. The best-known white wine is Locorotondo, named after the lovely hilltop town. In Matera every wine list will feature DOCG Aglianico del Vulture, the main wine of the region of Basilicata. It is a powerful and complex red from the Aglianico grape, which is grown in and around the extinct volcano Mount Vulture.

The cheapest wine in a restaurant is called the *vino della casa* (house wine). It is often served in jugs of a *litro* (litre) or *mezzo litro* (half litre). It is very variable and a great addition to any meal in the region.

When to eat

Italians traditionally eat lunch between noon and 3pm, and dinner no earlier than 7pm. Finding restaurants that will serve you between those hours might be tricky, especially in the less touristy areas.

Top 10 things to try

1. Orecchiette con cime di rapa
Puglia's most famous speciality bar none. This hand-made, ear-shaped pasta made with durum wheat semolina is known for its doughy and chewy texture and is most famously served with *cime di rapa*, or turnip tops, sautéed in oil, garlic and chilli – a very simple recipe with lots of flavour.

2. Burrata
This fresh cheese made with cow's milk, now known worldwide, is traditional of the Murge region. While the outer casing is made of solid cheese and resembles a large mozzarella, the inside is a soft and stringy mix of stracciatella and clotted cheese.

3. Friselle
They say that when the Phoenicians took off for their long journeys at sea, they would take along this dried bread, dipping it in sea water to soften it. Nowadays, *friselle* are softened with tap water

---

COOKERY COURSES

In Bari you can join a half-day walking tour combining sightseeing with a cookery class, learning how to make orecchiette from scratch. Lecce has the best choice of cookery courses, ranging from half a day to a week. The Awaiting Table (www.awaitingtable.com) offers week-long courses focusing on cookery and wine, held in Lecce or at a castle an hour south of the city. A shorter cookery course will typically include a visit to the market for local seasonal produce, a hands-on cookery class and a lunch or dinner with fine wines of Salento (see Cooking Experience, www.cookingexperience.it/en). Some of Puglia's wineries are open for tastings and tours; see the Puglia section at Winerist (www.winerist.com) for details and guided tours.

Friselle bread with tomatoes and olive oil

and seasoned with olive oil, tomatoes and olives for a refreshing and light summer meal.

4. Fave e cicoria

This broad bean purée, topped with chicory sautéed with oil and garlic, is omnipresent in every Puglian family meal and it's a common (and 100 percent vegan) appetizer featured on most restaurant menus.

5. Tiella

A close cousin to paella, the *tiella* dates back to the sixteenth century, when all of Southern Italy was under Spanish rule. It's a layered pie featuring potatoes, mussels, rice and onions, baked in the oven and served mainly in summer.

6. Focaccia barese

Puglia's answer to pizza is also one of the symbols of Apulian street food. Sold at any bakery, the *focaccia barese* is a soft flatbread made with flour and mashed potatoes for maximum fluffiness, topped with fresh tomatoes, olives and a sprinkle of oregano.

7. Cozze arraganate

This traditional seafood dish consists of fresh local mussels (*cozze*), halved and cleaned then stuffed with a gratin of breadcrumbs, olive oil, pecorino cheese and parsley, and baked in the oven.

8. Panzerotti

Also fittingly known as 'fried calzone', *panzerotti* are a local street food staple. They consist of hand-sized, half-moon-shaped pockets of pizza dough, traditionally filled with mozzarella and tomato (but also available with dozens of other fillings) and deep fried in seed oil.

9. Lampascioni

They look like small onions, but *lampascioni* are actually edible bulbs that grow locally. Normally served cooked or pickled with garlic, hot chilli, pepper and parsley, and used as a garnish or side dish for many foods.

10. Pasticciotti

A breakfast sweet that can be enjoyed all day long. This delicious and fragrant type of pastry traditionally comes filled with lemon-flavoured egg custard, but you'll find it in many different variants including chocolate or pistachio cream, ricotta or almond paste.

RICCI DI MARE

Well worth trying are *i ricci di mare* (sea urchins), available in spring and autumn. Locals tend to love them, tourists love or loathe them. Locally they are considered something of a delicacy because of the time it takes to collect them and the tiny amount of edible fish in each urchin. They are also tricky to open unless you have the right tool. The part you eat is often called the 'roe' but in fact it's the gonads that produce the eggs rather than the eggs themselves. In Bari you can buy them by the port, freshly caught and cracked open by the fishermen, so that you eat them raw – the fresher the better. Don't let the spiny exteriors put you off! They are also used to cook with pasta or risotto but don't be surprised if you only get a tiny quantity of the orange pulp on your pasta.

To help you order

A table for one/two/three **Un tavolo per una persona/per due/per tre**
I would like... **Vorrei...**
The bill, please. **Il conto, per favore.**
Do you have a set menu? **Avete un menù a prezzo fisso?**
I am allergic to **Sono allergico a…**
   …Gluten **Glutine**

beer **una birra**	pepper **del pepe**
bread **del pane**	potatoes **delle patate**
butter **del burro**	salad **un'insalata**
coffee **un caffè**	salt **del sale**
fish **del pesce**	soup **una minestra**
fruit **della frutta**	sugar **dello zucchero**
ice cream **un gelato**	tea **un tè**
meat **della carne**	water **dell'acqua**
milk **del latte**	wine **del vino**

Menu reader

aglio garlic	**maiale** pork
agnello lamb	**manzo** beef
aragosta lobster	**melanzane** aubergine
arancia orange	**merluzzo** cod
bistecca beefsteak	**ostriche** oysters
braciola chop	**pane** bread
calamari squid	**pollo** chicken
carciofi artichokes	**pomodori** tomatoes
cozze mussels	**prosciutto** ham
crostacei shellfish	**tacchino** turkey
fegato liver	**tonno** tuna
formaggio cheese	**uovo** egg
frutti di mare seafood	**verdure** vegetables
funghi mushrooms	**vongole** clams

Places to eat

Price for a two-course meal for one person, including a glass of wine and service charge:
€€€€ = over 50 euros
€€€ = 35–50 euros
€€ = 25–35 euros
€ = below 25 euros

The Gargano Peninsula

Monte Sant'Angelo

Medioevo Via Castello 21, www.ristorante-medioevo.it. In the historic centre (accessed by foot only) this excellent value restaurant focuses on local ingredients and regional specialities, including home-made pastas such as *troccoli* and aubergine *involtini* or *orecchiette medioevo,* pasta with rocket, pecorino and lamb. Good choice of Pugliese wines. €€

Peschici

Al Trabucco da Mimì Località Punta San Nicola, Peschici, www.altrabucco.it. Gorgeous spot on the sea and hugely popular for sunset *aperitivi*. Go for freshly cooked fish and seafood, and a very laidback atmosphere. Vegetarian options include *fave e cicorie*, broad beans and wild chicory. This is one of around a dozen *trabucchi* along the coast: wooden contraptions suspended over the sea, traditionally used to net fish. Closed winter. €€€€

Rodi Garganico

L'Operetta Osteria di Mare Largo Masaniello 10, Rodi Garganico, tel: 338 294 9480. Set on a square in the old town, this *osteria* has a spacious terrace overlooking the beach, harbour and sea. You won't have to agonise over the choice of dishes – it's either the fish or meat menu, both four courses with generous portions at low prices. Staff speak limited English. **€**

Vieste

Il Capriccio Località Porto Turistico, Vieste, www.ilcapricciovieste.it. Come for lovely harbour views and some superb fish creations from Chef Leonardo Vescera. Try monkfish in a pistachio and bread crust with orange and cherry sauce or fresh ravioli with sea urchins and *burrata* (creamy mozzarella), followed by one of the sumptuous desserts. There is also a sushi bar and a wine bar. **€€€**

Puglia Imperiale

Trani

Quintessenza Via Lionelli 62, www.quintessenzaristorante.it. Splash out here on some of the best cuisine in southern Italy. Innovative interpretations of classic Puglian dishes – all artfully presented – have earned self-taught Stefano a Michelin star. For a range of specialities opt for one of the tasting menus with wine pairings. Expect the likes of ceviche of grouper with plums and rhubarb, marinated amberjack with tomato and beetroot or *tortelli* with ricotta, red prawns and Trani Muscat bisque. **€€€€**

Bari and beyond

Bari

L'Osteria del Borgo Antico Piazza Mercantile 15, tel: 080 521 0124, mobile: 335 7709 805. A buzzing and friendly *osteria* on the beautiful Piazza

Mercantile, with an outdoor terrace for watching the world go by. Starters include a delicious selection of antipasti to share, pastas feature Puglian specials such as *cavatelli* and *orecchiette*, or try the regional speciality of *patate, riso e cozze* (potatoes, rice and mussels). Fresh fish includes *gamberini*, cuttlefish on a skewer or delicious grilled seabass. They serve good pizzas too, which go down well with the house Primitivo. Closed Wednesdays. €€

Panificio Fiore Strada Palazzo di Città 38, tel: 080 523 6290. Just behind the Basilica di San Nicola this is a bakery rather than a restaurant but it's a great spot for *focaccia,* fresh from the oven, either classic tomato or other flavours. It's one of the oldest and most popular bakeries in Bari – so be prepared to queue. Buy a beer (sold here) and take your snack to one of the benches on the seafront. €

Polignano a Mare

Mint Cucina Fresca Via San Benedetto 32, http://mintcucinafresca.com/. A shabby chic location with just a few tables and a fairly relaxed atmosphere, offering fresh fish dishes alongside a wide selection of vegan offerings including raw courgette noodles with avocado and mint pesto, onion quiche made with chickpea dough, and a variety of tofu specialities. €€

Savelletri

Ristorante Albachiara Contrada Lamascopone, Fasano, http://lamascopone.it. On the rocky coast between Savelletri and Torre Canne, this is a laidback, fairly basic place with a glorious setting overlooking the turquoise sea. Try specialities such as the tender grilled octopus, mixed seafood or home-made pasta with sea urchins, accompanied by the house rosé. Waiters are friendly and it's a good spot for a family seaside lunch. €€

Valle d'Itria

Alberobello

L'Aratro Via Monte San Michele 25–29, Alberobello, www.ristorantearatro.it/en. Don't be put off by the touristy street, in the main *trulli* quarter of Alberobello. This is a characterful, rustic restaurant, converted from a complex of *trulli* and with a garden for dining at the back. Specialising in slow food, it offers an excellent range of Puglian specialities displaying names of the local providers. Starters feature local cheeses and *salumi* or seafood from the Adriatic. For pasta try *cavatellucci di Terra Madre,* pasta with cherry tomatoes, red onions and diced *capocollo* (dry-cured pork), served on a bed of mashed broad beans and wild chicory. Wine labels number around a hundred – mainly from local vineyards. €€€

Ceglie Messapica

Osteria Pugliese Vico I, Orto Nanna Vecchia 10, Ceglie Messapica, tel: 0831 377 115. It's unsurprising that this no-frills, family-run *osteria* in the historical centre is packed with locals. Prices are exceptionally low for the authentic local fare and the atmosphere is homely and congenial. Don't miss out on the antipasti – almost a meal in itself with around a dozen dishes including regional cheeses, charcuterie and vegetables. €

Cisternino

Da Zio Pietro Via Duca d'Aosta 3, Cisternino, tel: 080 444 8300. Carnivores will love this butcher-cum-deli-cum-restaurant in the charming hilltop town of Cisternino. You choose your locally sourced meat to be cooked in a wood-burning oven, then tuck in at tables inside or out and wash it down with remarkably cheap house wine. This has been a family butcher business since 1935 and it is very popular. Get there in the early evening or be prepared to queue. Dinner only; no bookings are taken. €€

Martina Franca

Garibaldi Bistrot Piazza Plebiscito 13, Martina Franca, tel: 080 483 7987, www.facebook.com/garibaldibistrot. The setting overlooking the Basilica di San Martino, the friendly, helpful service, flavoursome dishes and favourable prices make this one of the most popular restaurants in the centre. Don't miss the house antipasti with creamy *burrata* cheese, cured meats, vegetarian, vegan and other local dishes which keep flowing from the kitchen (one between two is plenty!). €€€

Macelleria Braceria Granaldi Via Vincenzo Bellini 108, Martina Franca, tel: 080 698 7892, www.facebook.com/braceria.granaldi. Carnivores look no further. Choose your meat to be grilled from the butcher's counter and enjoy it, cooked for you, in the simple little restaurant upstairs or outside on the street. The choice includes succulent steaks, tender roast lamb, belly pork slices, slow-cooked offal and *bombette* – little pork rolls filled with more meat, cheese, and breadcrumbs and cooked on a skewer. It all goes down well with a bottle of Primitivo di Manduria. Dinner only; closed Sundays. €€

Nausikaa Vico Arco Fumarola 2, Martina Franca, www.ristorantenausikaa.it. This gem of a restaurant, on a side street of the old town, is run by brothers Martino and Francesco whose early training in Puglian cuisine came from their grandmother many years ago. Their bold and imaginative interpretations of traditional Salentine dishes, all beautifully presented, live up to the brothers' maxim: *Trasformiamo il cibo in poesia* (We transform food into poetry). Closed Mondays. €€€

Ostuni

Osteria del Tempo Perso Via Gaetano Tanzarella Vitale 47, Ostuni, www.osteriadeltempoperso.com. In the historic centre of Ostuni, this long-established *osteria* is divided into two dining areas, one of which is an evocative 500-year-old cave, formerly used as a bakery. Cured meat from Martina Franca, stuffed cuttlefish or *burrata* cheese with pomegranate can be followed by local pastas such as *orecchiette* with clams and courgette flowers or wholewheat *strascinate* pasta with *cime di rapa* (broccoli rabe), anchovies and breadcrumbs. Mains include seabass and steak and there are also vegetarian and gluten-free dishes. Reservations are advisable, particularly for cave-dining. €€€€

Salento

Brindisi

Cozza Nera Via Schiavone 19, Angolo via Appia, tel: 0831 560 752, www.facebook.com/cozzanera. Come for generous helpings of simple fish dishes such as *frittura mista* (mixed fried fish), *riso con patate e cozze* (rice with potatoes and mussels) or *spigola in crosta di mandorle* (seabass in an almond crust), prepared in front of you and served on plastic plates or silver foil trays. Good choice for a quick bite. Fish only. Closed Mondays. €€

Gallipoli

Matre Via Antonietta de Pace 116, Gallipoli, tel: 0833 264430, www.instagram.com/matreristorante. For fine dining in the centre of Gallipoli look no further. It's well worth splashing out on the seven-course fish tasting menu comprising five antipasti, including the local purple shrimps (*gamberi viola*), a pasta, perhaps *tortelli* with lobster, plus a dessert. Dinner only. €€€

Lecce

Alle due Corti Corte dei Giugni 1 (corner of Via Prato), Lecce, www.alleduecorti.com. Famous for the now fashionable *cucina povera* (food of the poor), this eatery is run by renowned chef, Rosalba De Carlo. Her ancient Salentine dishes are based on the humblest of ingredients: *ciceri and tria* (pasta with chickpeas), *fave nette cu le cicureddhe* (broad bean purée with wild chicory) and *taieddha* (mussels, potatoes and rice, baked in the oven) – all washed down with jugs of Negroamaro house wine. Rosalba also offers cooking courses, see the website for more information. Closed Sundays. €€

Trattoria Le Zie Via Colonnello Archimede Costadura 19, Lecce, tel: 0832 245178. The small, quaint dining room, full of pictures and photos and dating back to 1966, feels like a family home and is popular with locals. The aunts (*le zie*) produce authentic, home-made food with simple dishes such as meatballs (a real favourite), fava bean purée with chicory, stuffed squid or stewed octopus. It is very popular so book in advance – if you don't speak any Italian ask a local to do it for you. Closed Mondays and Sundays. €

Otranto

L'Alternativa Pizzeria Ristorante Via Padre Scupoli 14, Otranto, tel: 338 377 9684, www.facebook.com/lalternativapizzeria.otranto. A simple but delicious dining option in the historic center. Alongside the perfectly baked Puglian pizzas with their thin dough and crunchy crust, this restaurant also serves pastas and a variety of fried fish options. Great value. €

LaltroBaffo Via Cenobio Basiliano 23, Otranto, www.laltrobaffo.com. Tuck into raw or cooked fish antipasti, a renowned carbonara of sea urchins or a platter of prawns, langoustines and local lobster at this small, family-run restaurant. Young chef Cristina Conte, along with her mother and sister, produce creative new versions of traditional Salentine seafood recipes. The setting is simple and stylish, with a small terrace for alfresco dining. €€€

Basilicata

Matera

L'Abbondanza Lucana Via Bruno Buozzi 11, Sasso Caveoso, Matera, tel: 0835 334574. Take a tour of Basilicata cuisine with the *antipasti misti* and you will realise why this restaurant is called '*L'Abbondanza Lucana*' (Abundance from Basilicata). The antipasti, home-made pasta and mains, which include slow-cooked pork cheeks and tender wild boar, go well with the local, full-bodied Aglianico del Vulture wine, dubbed 'the Barolo of the south'. The setting is an elegant series of caves, with a terrace for outdoor eating. Closed Mondays and Sundays. €€€

Alle Fornaci Piazza Firrao, 7, www.ristorantealleffornaci.it. This soberlooking spot in the new town is one of the few places in Matera to specialise in seafood. Dishes are traditionally prepared but come with a gourmet twist, such as *baccalà con polenta* (cod with polenta) or squid ink *orecchiette* with artichoke cream, cuttlefish and lime. A great little restaurant for a delicious meal. €€€

Baccus Vico Santa Cesarea 34 (Angolo Via D'Addozio), Matera, www.ristorantebaccus.it. On the edge of Matera's Sassi (ancient cave-dwellings), *Baccus* has a romantic partial-cave setting as well as outdoor tables set across a rustic terrace. The superb house antipasti is enough for a whole meal for two, which consists of cheeses, cured meats, *peperoni cruschi* (crushed peppers) and ricotta soufflé. For a pasta, try the Aglianico wine dough bavette pasta with caciocavallo cheese cream, pepper, pistachios and *crusco* pepper chips. It all goes down well with the house Primitivo wine, so order a glass while you tuck into your food. Closed Mondays. €€

Travel essentials

Practical information

Accessible travel	**128**
Accommodation	**128**
Airports	**129**
Apps	**129**
Bicycle rental	**130**
Budgeting	**130**
Camping	**131**
Car hire	**131**
Climate	**132**
Crime and safety	**132**
Driving	**133**
Electricity	**134**
Embassies and consulates	**134**
Emergencies	**134**
Getting there	**134**
Guides and tours	**135**
Health and medical care	**135**
Language	**136**
LGBTQ+ travellers	**136**
Money	**136**
Opening hours	**137**
Police	**137**
Public holidays	**138**
Telephone	**138**
Time zones	**139**
Tipping	**139**
Toilets	**139**
Tourist information	**139**
Transport	**140**
Visa and entry requirements	**141**

Accessible travel

Puglia can present problems for travellers with disabilities. The hilltop towns have steep cobbled streets, many churches and sites have steps and some museums do not have wheelchair access. Given the challenges it is wisest to book through a specialised tour operator or travel agency who can offer customized tours and itineraries, for example Disabled Holidays (www.disabledholidays.com).

Accommodation

Puglia has plentiful accommodation ranging from stylish boutique hotels and villas to simple B&Bs and farms. For peaceful getaways there is the option of *masserie*, traditional farmhouses which have been restored and converted into tourist accommodation. In the last twenty years or so these have been very much part of the rapid rise in tourism in Puglia. They range from basic *agriturismo*-style family farms to sophisticated five-star hotels, often in rustic style, with suites in villas and outbuildings, a peaceful pool and perhaps a private beach, golf course and/or spa treatments. Most lie within fifteen minutes' drive or so from nearby towns or attractions but they are typically in seemingly remote locations amid olive groves and vineyards. A hired car is advisable, especially if you don't intend to dine in every evening. Most of the *masserie* serve meals, often sumptuous ones featuring Puglian specialities with food sourced straight from the farm or from small local suppliers. Many of Puglia's iconic *trulli* (see page 60) in the Valle d'Itria have also been converted to guest accommodation, with modern-day facilities. These squat conical houses range from deluxe conversions to something more akin to the original peasant-farmer dwelling. B&Bs and Airbnbs are plentiful in Puglia. Simple self-catering facilities are often provided which can save on restaurant costs and enable those with specific dietary requirements to choose and cook their own ingredients.

During the high season accommodation in popular resorts along the coast should be booked ahead, especially in July and August. Prices drop dramatically off-season (between 30 and 50 percent) and moving away from the coast, but bear in mind that many resorts close in winter.

For details of *agriturismi*, *masserie* and other rural accommodation go to the Puglia section of Agriturismo.net (www.agriturismo.net). Charming Puglia (www.charmingpuglia.com/en) have a decent selection of excellent hotels, *trulli* and *masserie* to browse through.

Airports

Bari's **Karol Wojtyla Airport**, named after the late Pope John Paul II and also known as Palese Airport (www.aeroportidipuglia.it), is 10km (6 miles) northwest of Bari city centre. Terravision in conjunction with Autoservizi Tempesta provide a shuttle bus service to Central Station in Bari (€4 one way) which takes about 30min and operates from 05.10am to 12.40am. Tickets can be bought on board the bus. AMTAB Line 16 is the cheapest bus service (€1 one way) but slower (about 40min), with frequent stops. Tickets can be purchased from the newsagent inside the terminal building. Bari airport is on the metropolitan rail service (the FM2 line) which takes just twenty minutes to get to Bari central station but it is a good 10min walk to the station from the airport through a series of tunnels. Trains run from 05.26am to 11.38pm every 20 or 30 minutes. Tickets (€5 one-way) can be bought online at www.ferrovienordbarese.it or at the station. Pugliairbus (www.aeroportidipuglia.it; click on Bari then transport) connects the airports of Bari, Brindisi, Foggia and Taranto, also to Matera in Basilicata. A taxi to the centre of Bari from the airport takes 20–25 minutes and costs around €25.

Brindisi's **Salento Airport** (www.aeroportidipuglia.it) is a small airport 4km (2.5 miles) from the city centre. Ryanair is currently the only airline flying directly from the UK (out of Stansted and Manchester). A bus runs into the city centre every 30min, taking around half an hour (€4). There is also a direct and cheap bus service to Lecce. A taxi (€20) takes around 15min to the centre.

Apps

For taxis, download the Italian taxi app **itTaxi**. The tourist office's official app, **Visit Puglia**, suggests nearby sights such as hamlets, museums, beaches and more, and is a great resource when driving around the region. For a more creative approach, popular app **Sherazade** recounts the histories and stories of many of Puglia's sights.

Bicycle rental

See also Sustainable Travel, page 11. Cycle-hire is widely available and an increasing number of hotels have bikes for guests' use. Scooters, mopeds and electric bikes as well as trekking, road and hybrid bikes can be hired in most towns and resorts. Tourist information offices can supply names and prices of bike-hire places. Rental costs are typically €15–20 for a day, €35–€45 for three days. Electric bikes are available at an extra cost. Bikes can be taken on regional train services displaying the bike logo but you need to buy a bike ticket. Puglia in Movimento (www.pugliainmovimento.com) is a Bari bike service with free delivery to the airport, railway station or your hotel, also offering assistance on self-guided bike tours, tour guides, moving luggage day by day and other services. Alternatively, the official tourism website Viaggiare in Puglia offers booklets with itineraries for independent cyclists (https://viaggiareinpuglia.it/en/area-download).

Budgeting

Flight prices to Puglia vary hugely, depending on the season, the day of the week and how far in advance you book. A return flight from the UK to Bari with a low-cost carrier costs around €100 in winter, €200–300 in high season (basic flight prices). For a real bargain look for last minute offers, sometimes at ridiculously low prices.

A double room in a budget hotel will cost €60–120 per night, in a mid-range hotel €100–250 and for a luxury *masseria* in high season you can pay as much as €400–700. B&Bs, Airbnb and *agriturismi* offer much cheaper accommodation and youth hostels charge €15–25 in a dorm or from €30 for a basic double room. Restaurants in popular resorts, especially with a sea view, might set you back €45 for a three-course dinner with wine, rising to over €100 for one of the top restaurants. Simple trattorias charge much less. Fuel costs are similar to those across Europe but public transport remains inexpensive.

Coffee served at a table costs €1.50–3, a coke or soft drink €2.50–3, a beer €2.50–4, a glass of wine from €3–5, cocktails €6–10. If all you need is to quench your thirst remember that, in the more touristy areas, drinks at the bar are cheaper than those served on the terrace.

Museum entrance fees vary from €3–20. Visitors under 18 are entitled to free admission to state museums, those aged 18–25 from the EU are entitled to reduced price tickets. Combined tickets to several sights are available in the major cities. The main centres, such as Bari and Lecce, offer free guided tours of the city.

Camping

Camping is only permitted in designated sites. Many of the campsites are vast recreational centres with restaurants, pools, bars and sports facilities, often close to the sea. The majority are only open for the summer season, either from April to October or June to September. Local tourist offices can provide details of sites in the region. For those who don't have their own tent or caravan there are bungalows and static caravans to rent, but it is advisable to book ahead. For details of sites consult Camping.it (www.camping.it/en) or Campeggi.com (www.campeggi.com/en).

Car hire

Hiring a car is by far the easiest way to explore Puglia, though driving in the towns and cities is not for the faint-hearted. Most major companies such as Avis, Hertz and Europcar have outlets at the airports but it is usually cheaper to book in advance. It's also worth checking the car rental offers that appear when booking flights with low-cost airlines, as they sometimes have good offers. Car rental costs from around £300 per week for a small car. 'Inclusive' prices do not generally include personal accident insurance or insurance against damage to windscreens, tyres and wheels. Optional excess insurance costs from around €15 a day – it is far cheaper to take out your own excess insurance policy in advance. The minimum age for hiring a car is 21–25, depending on the company, and anyone hiring must have held a valid licence for at least one year. Rental companies will accept your country's national driving licence but you must show your passport or ID. Credit cards are taken as a deposit and are usually the only form of payment acceptable. Cards needs to be issued in the name of the first driver. Some car rental companies won't accept American Express at the counter, so Amex users should check with the company in advance or plan to use a different card. Beware of companies trying to overcharge for petrol when you take the car back, claiming the tank is not full on return. Keep your last petrol receipt just in case you need to challenge them.

Car-hire companies:
Avis www.avis.com
Budget www.budget.com
Europcar www.europcar.com
Hertz www.hertz.com
Sixt www.sixt.com

Climate

The heat in July and August can be relentless and it's not unusual for daytime temperatures to soar to 40°C (95°F). If you go at this time of year make sure you are close either to a beach or a swimming pool and do as the Italians do and take a siesta in the afternoon. The best times from the point of view of climate and fewer tourists are spring (April–early June), with the added bonus of a profusion of blossom and wildflowers, and early autumn (September–October) after the crowds have gone but while the air and sea are still warm. But beware that the season is short and by late September many coastal hotels and resorts have closed down for winter. The wettest months are from November to February, but rainfall is rarely significant.

Crime and safety

Take precautions against pickpockets, especially in ports such as Bari and Brindisi and take extra care in Taranto. Leave passports, jewellery, large amounts of cash, credit cards you are not using and other valuables in the hotel room safe – if it has one. Keep a copy of your passport and other valuable documents separately in case you need to replace them. Be particularly vigilant at markets, street festivals and on public transport. To protect yourself against Vespa-riding bandits who snatch bags while whizzing by at high speed, carry your bag so it faces away from the street. Never leave valuables in view within your car. If you are robbed report it as soon as possible to the local police. You will need a copy of the declaration in order to claim on your insurance.

Driving

You do not need an International Driving Permit to drive in the EU if you have a photocard driving licence issued in the UK. The network of roads across the region has much improved though you can still expect potholes on some roads. The main frustrations are negotiating town centres (poor signing to the centre, complex one-way systems and congested streets), finding parking places, following diversion signs (often to avoid town centres) which disappear and keeping your cool with fellow motorists who drive fast and sometimes recklessly.

Rules and regulations. The speed limit on motorways is 130km/h (80mph), on secondary roads 90km/h (55mph), in towns 50km/h (30mph). Drive on the right, overtake on the left. At intersections and roundabouts traffic on the right has priority. Speeding and other traffic offences are subject to heavy on-the-spot fines. The use of hand-held mobiles while driving is prohibited. The blood alcohol limit is 0.05 percent (the UK limit is 0.08 percent) and police occasionally make random breath tests.

Breakdowns and assistance. In case of an accident or breakdown, dial 113 (general emergency) or the Automobile Club of Italy on 116. Roadside phones are placed at frequent intervals along major roads.

Parking. Historic centres are often inaccessible to cars, other than those of residents. Look out for ZTL (*zona a traffico limitato*) signs at the entrance to restricted traffic areas, enforced with cameras. You can enter only if you are staying at accommodation within the restricted zone and you have a special permission document, and it is often the case that you can only drop off your luggage, before finding a parking place outside the centre. Enquire in advance from your hotel or B&B. If driving into a historic centre during high season (and in some towns out of it too) the hotel will need to take your registration number and inform the police. Many cities and towns have municipal parking lots and garages, denoted by a white 'P' on a blue background, at the fringes of their historic centres.

Petrol. Petrol and diesel are readily available. Diesel is called *diesel* or *gasolio*, petrol *benzina senza piombo* (also *benzina verde*). Many stations have self-service pumps, available 24 hours.

Electricity

220V/50Hz is standard. Visitors from other countries may require an adaptor and those from North America will need a transforrner as well. Sockets are either two- or three round-pins.

Embassies and consulates

Australian Embassy Via Antonio Bosio 5, Rome; tel: 06 852 721; http://italy.embassy.gov.au
Canadian Consulate Via Zara 30, Rome; tel: 06 854441; www.canada.it
Irish Embassy Villa Spada, Via Giacomo Medici 1, Rome; tel: 06 585 2381; www.dfa.ie/irish-embassy/italy
Honorary Consulate of South Africa Via Beata Elia di San Clemente, 255, 72122 Bari; tel: 080 524 0388; email: consolato.sudafrica.bari@gmail.com
UK Embassy Via XX Settembre 80a, Rome; tel: 06 4220 0001; www.gov.uk/world/organisations/british-embassy-rome
US Embassy Via Vittorio Veneto 121, Rome; tel: 06 46741; https://it.usembassy.gov

Emergencies

The general emergency number is **113**. Call **112** for police, **115** for fire and **118** for an ambulance. For road assistance call **116**.

Getting there

Before travelling visitors from the UK should check the entry requirements for Italy at https://www.gov.uk/foreign-travel-advice/italy.

Air travel. Puglia is served by low-cost charter and scheduled airlines from the UK and other parts of Europe. British Airways operates flights from Heathrow to Bari and Brindisi; Ryanair flies from London Stansted to Bari daily, and to Brindisi three times a week in season, twice a week in winter; easyJet runs flights from Gatwick to both airports.

Guides and tours

Day-trip itineraries with multilingual guides are available through hotels, tourist offices, local travel agencies and tour operators. In Bari there are guided walking, biking and rickshaw tours, often combining culture with street food. The city has a lively mp3 audio guide combined with a map. Popular destinations for guided day-trips are Lecce for Baroque splendour, Alberobello for quaint *trulli*, Castellana Grotte for spectacular caves and Matera in Basilicata for cave dwellings. Gastronomy is the theme of many tours throughout Puglia, perhaps making (and eating) your own Puglian pasta (see page 115), visiting an oil press or vineyards with tastings along the way. The official Puglia tourist website (www.viaggiareinpuglia.it) has details of guided tours and websites of operators.

Health and medical care

The Italian Tourist Board website (http://italia.it) has details of regulations for travelling within Italy and for access to recreational activities and services. Visitors should carry with them the EHIC (European Health Insurance Card) or the GHIC (UK Global Health Insurance Card). The GHIC card is available for free in the UK from the NHS website (www.nhs.uk/using-the-nhs/healthcare-abroad) which entitles you to free medical treatment within the EU. Existing EHIC cards remain valid until the expiry date, after which you need to apply for a GHIC card. The cards cover only medical care, not emergency repatriation costs or additional expenses. It is therefore important to have travel insurance to cover all eventualities. Should you be asked to pay for treatment up front, keep all receipts for reimbursement. In many areas in summer there is a Guardia Medica Turistica (tourist emergency medical service) which functions 24 hours a day. Details are available from pharmacies, tourist offices, hotels and local newspapers.

Pharmacies (*farmacie*) have a green cross sign above the entrance. In each town, one stays open late and on Sundays on a rotating basis. The after-hour locations for the month are posted on the doors of all pharmacies. For serious cases or **emergencies**, dial 118 for an ambulance or head for the *Pronto Soccorso* (Accident and Emergency) department of the local hospital.

Tap water is safe to drink.

Language

English is spoken in hotels and restaurants of main towns and resorts, but once you venture off the tourist track, prepare to communicate in Italian. Standard Italian is spoken throughout the region, but, as elsewhere in Italy, Puglia has its own dialects. One of the most notable is *griko,* a dialect of Greek which is very occasionally spoken by the older generation in the 'Greek villages' of Grecia Salentina, south of Lecce.

LGBTQ+ travellers

Attitudes are more relaxed nowadays and there are LGBTQ+ hangouts in the main cities, especially Bari where it's easy to find LGBTQ+ clubs, saunas and cruising spots. Gallipoli is another popular LGBTQ+ centre, which hosts Salento Pride in mid-August. There are a handful of LGBTQ+ beaches in Puglia, mainly in the Salento region and including Gallipoli. The national LGBTQ+ rights organisation is Arci-gay (www.arcigay.it). Gay Friendly Italy (www.gayfriendlyitaly.com) is an English-language website for LGBTQ+ travellers in Italy and includes venues in Puglia.

Money

Currency. The currency in Italy is the euro (€). A euro is divided into 100 cents with 2, 5, 10, 20 and 50 cent coins, and 1 and 2 euro coins. The euro notes are 5, 10, 20, 50, 100, 200 and 500.

Currency exchanges. Money can be changed at exchange offices and some banks and post offices. Exchange offices (*cambios*) are found in most towns and have the longest opening hours, but banks and post offices normally offer the best rates of exchange.

Credit cards. Visa and Master Card are the most widely accepted credit cards, and many establishments do not take American Express. Nowadays, major credit cards are widely accepted in shops, hotels, restaurants and petrol stations. Some museums and churches might insist on cash. Cards can also be used to pay motorway tolls, but it is advisable also to keep some cash on-hand, as the card-reading machines are sometimes out of order.

Opening hours

Opening hours of museums, galleries, churches and castles vary widely. Churches are usually closed from noon to 4 or 5pm but don't be surprised to find monuments closed for ongoing restoration or major sites closed without warning. Local tourist boards can provide current opening times for sights in their town or region.

Banks. Mon–Fri 8.30am–1pm or 1.30pm and most are also open 2.30/3pm–4/4.30pm.

Shops. Mon–Sat 8 or 9am–1pm and 4–7.30/8pm, but many non-food shops close on Monday and, with the exception of supermarkets, food shops may close on Wednesday. In main towns and resorts some shops stay open at lunchtime and on Sundays.

Museums. Opening hours vary and constantly change. Most museums are open six days a week, the most common closing day being Monday. Some museums open mornings only on Sundays and holidays.

Police

There are three kinds of police in Italy: the *vigili urbani*, who deal with petty crime, traffic, parking and other local, day-to-day matters; the *carabinieri* who are the armed military police who handle law and order and the *polizia stradale* who patrol the roadways. Any of these forces may answer a 113 emergency call, though the *carabinieri* have their own emergency number, 112.

Public holidays

Banks and most shops are closed on the following holidays:

January 1 New Year's Day (*Capodanno*)
January 6 Epiphany (*Epifania*)
March/April Easter Sunday and Monday (*Pasqua e Pasquetta*)
April 25 Liberation Day (*Festa della Liberazione*)
May 1 Labour Day (*Festa del Lavoro*)
June 2 Republic Day (*Festa della Repubblica*)
August 15 Assumption Day (*Ferragosto*)
November 1 All Saints' Day (*Ognissanti*)
December 8 Immaculate Conception (*Immacolata Concezione*)
December 25 Christmas Day (*Natale*)
December 26 Boxing Day (*Festa di Santo Stefano*)

Telephone

To call an Italian telephone number from outside Italy, either from a landline or mobile, you need to add the international dialling code for Italy which is 0039 (+39), followed by the telephone number you require, including the first 0. For calls within Italy, telephone numbers must be preceded by the area code even if the call is made within the same district. When phoning abroad from Italy dial 00 (the international access code), then the country code, followed by the city or area code omitting the initial 0, and then the desired number. Hotels levy large surcharges on long-distance calls.

Mobile (cell) phones. Since the UK left the EU the guarantee of free roaming for UK mobile users has ended. It is now up to the network provider to decide whether to charge international roaming rates and if so, how much. Check with your company prior to departure. By law customers must be informed when they have used up 80 percent and 100 percent of their data allowance. There is also a rule whereby they cannot be charged more than £45 of mobile data charges, unless they have actively opted to continue using data when abroad. If you are being charged and you are making a large number of calls or staying for some time it may be worth purchasing a 'pay as you go' SIM card (*una scheda ricaricabile*) available at shops of the main providers or at post offices.

Time zones

Italy is one hour ahead of Greenwich Mean Time (GMT). From the last Sunday in March to the last Sunday in October, clocks are put forward by one hour. The chart below shows times across the globe when it is midday in Bari.

New York	**Puglia**	Jo'burg	Sydney	Auckland
7am	**noon**	1pm	9pm	11pm

Tipping

In Italy a service charge of 10–15 percent is usually built into the bill, though a little extra for good service is always welcome. At a bar, leaving a coin or two on the counter for a barman is appreciated. Tip porters one euro per bag. To tip a taxi driver simply round up the total to the nearest euro or two.

Toilets

Public toilets are hard to find, but you can usually use toilets in cafés and bars. In some cases the toilets are locked and you will have to ask for the key (*la chiave*). Buying a drink at the same time will be appreciated. Major sites now have reasonable facilities. The men's toilets are signed *Uomini* or *Signori*, the ladies' *Donne* or *Signore*.

Tourist information

The website for the Italian National Tourist Board (ENIT) is www.enit.it. The official tourism website for Puglia is www.viaggiareinpuglia.it.

The main tourist offices in Puglia will have staff who speak English but this is often not the case with the smaller information offices. Normal opening hours are daily, all day during the summer, but off-season hours are much shorter. A travel agency or local tour operator can be a good source of advice if the tourist office is closed or non-existent. The following are the tourist offices in the main towns:

Puglia
Alberobello Via Monte Nero 1, tel: 379 298 7173 (WhatsApp too)
Bari Piazza Ferrarese 29, tel: 331 5452520
Brindisi Via Duomo 20, tel: 0831 229784
Gallipoli Via Kennedy 20, tel: 0833 264283
Lecce c/o Sedile Comunale, Piazza Sant'Oronzo, tel: 0832 242099
Martina Franca Piazza XX Settembre 3, tel: 0804 411 65 54
Ostuni Corso Mazzini 8, tel: 0831 1982471
Otranto c/o Castello Aragonese, Piazza Castello, tel: 0836 212747
Taranto Castello Aragonese, tel: 334 2844 098
Trani Piazza Trieste 10, tel: 3755575405
Vieste Piazza Kennedy 13, tel: 0884 708806

Basilicata
Matera Piazza Vittorio Veneto, tel: 0835 680254

Transport
Coach and bus. Bus services, operated by around twenty different companies, link Puglia's main towns and offer relatively speedy access across the region. Generally speaking, coaches are more reliable and quicker than trains and for small towns are often the only option. For details of the different companies and their destinations consult the official tourist website, www.viaggiareinpuglia.it, under the Useful Info section. Note that there are far fewer services on Sundays and holidays.

Ferry. Three ferry companies service the Tremiti Islands, off the coast of the Gargano Peninsula. These are GS Travel (www.gstravel.eu/en), Navi Tremiti (www.navitremiti.com) and NavLib (www.navlib.it). Boats depart to the islands from various points on the coast, including Vieste and Peschici in summer. The only year-round service is from Termoli in Molise.

Helicopter. You can fly to the Tremiti Islands from Foggia by helicopter with Alidaunia (www.alidaunia.it).

Rail. Trains are operated by Trenitalia (www.trenitalia.com). The system is cheap but there are fewer high-speed trains and tracks than in the north and the system is often slower and less convenient than journeys by bus or coach for seeing the region. Main stations have self-service ticket machines with instructions in English and this is usually quicker than using the ticket office. Tickets can also be bought online. Travel on InterCity and the high-speed Frecciarossa, Frecciargento and Frecciabianca trains is faster on longer stretches, but also more expensive. Tickets for all trains must be stamped in the yellow machines on the platforms before boarding the train. Failure to do so can incur a hefty on-the-spot fine. Puglia has four regional private lines: Ferrovie del Sud Est (www.fseonline.it) connecting Bari and its south-east province to Brindisi, Lecce and Taranto; Ferrovie Appulo Lucane (www.ferrovieappulolucane.it) running across the province of Bari and the Murgia towns to Basilicata; Ferrotramviaria (www.ferrovienordbarese.it) connecting Bari to its main northern province towns and the Barletta-Andria-Trani province and finally Ferrovie del Gargano (www.ferroviedelgargano.com) serving the whole province of Foggia. Tourist offices can provide a free and useful leaflet with a map of the different services, as can helpdesks within stations. Note that outside high season the train services to popular resorts tend to be less frequent, so check ahead.

Taxi. In cities taxis can be found in main squares, or can be telephoned. The meter should be turned on at the start of the journey. Beware of touts without meters who may approach you at airports and large train stations.
Bari: Radio Taxi, tel: 080 554 3333
Lecce: Radio Taxi, tel: 331 241 0613

Visa and entry requirements

For current entry requirements to Italy, including rules regarding health concerns, UK citizens should consult www.gov.uk/foreign-travel-advice/italy/entry-requirements. A British passport is sufficient for stays in Italy for up to ninety days. Citizens of the US, Canada, Australia, New Zealand and South Africa also need only a valid passport for stays of no more than ninety days. Visitors should ensure their passport is valid for at least six months beyond the departure date.

Index

A
Abbazia di Santa Maria di Cerrate 76
accessible travel 128
accommodation 128
airports 129
Alberobello 61
    Rione Aia Piccola 62
    Rione Monti 61
    Trullo Sovrano 62
Andria 45
apps 129

B
Bari 53
    Bari Vecchia 54
    Basilica di San Nicola 56
    Castello Normanno Svevo 54
    Cattedrale di San Sabino 55
    Chiesa di San Gregorio 56
    Museo del Succorpo della Cattedrale 55
    Piazza Mercantile 57
Barletta 45
bicycle rental 130
Brindisi 69
    Duomo 70
    Monumento Al Marinaio d'Italia 70
    Museo Archeologico Provinciale Ribezzo 70
    Palazzo Granafei-Nervegna 70
    Roman Column 70
    Scalinata Virgiliana 70
    Tempio di San Giovanni al Sepolcro 70
budgeting 130

C
Calimera 77
camping 131
Canne della Battaglia 47
    Antiquarium 47
    Parco Archeologico di Canne della Battaglia 47
Canosa di Puglia 47
Capocollo di Martina Franca 63
car hire 131
Castel del Monte 44
Castro 82
Cattedrale di San Sabino 48
Chiesa del Santo Sepolcro 46
Cisternino 65
climate 132
Colossus 45
Corigliano d'Otranto 77
crime and safety 132

D
driving 133

E
Egnazia 59
electricity 134
embassies and consulates 134
emergencies 134

F
Foggia 42
Fondazione Museo Pino Pascali 58
Foresta Umbra 34
Frederick II 46

G
Galatina 78
Gallipoli 83
    bastions 84
    Castello Angioino 84
    Cattedrale di Sant'Agata 84
    fish market 84
    Frantoio Ipogeo 84
Grotta Bianca 61
Grottaglie 87
Grotte di Castellana 60
guides and tours 135

I
Il Tavoliere 42
Isole Tremiti 40

L
La Grotta Zinzulusa 82
language 136
La Notte della Taranta 77
Lecce 71
    Basilica di San Giovanni Battista 75
    Basilica di Santa Croce 73
    Chiesa di Santa Chiara 75
    Duomo 75
    Museo Archeologico

Faggiano 75
Piazza del Duomo 74
Piazza Sant'Oronzo 72
Roman amphitheatre 72
Sedile 73
LGBTQ+ travellers 136
Locorotondo 62
Lucera 42

M

Marina di Pescoluse 83
Martina Franca 63
Chiesa di San Martino 64
Palazzo Ducale 64
Piazza Plebiscito 64
Piazza XX Settembre 64
Porto Santo Stefano 64
Matera 88
Casa-Grotta di Vico Solitario 93
Cattedrale di Matera 93
Chiesa di Madonna delle Virtù 92
Chiesa di San Nicola dei Greci 92
Chiesa di Santa Lucia alle Malve 92
Chiesa San Pietro Barisano 91
Chiesa Santa Maria de Idris 92
Palombaro Lungo 93
Parco della Murgia Materana 93
Piazza Vittorio Veneto 93
San Giovanni in Monterrone 92

Sasso Barisano 91
Sasso Caveoso 92
money 136
Monopoli 59
Monte Sant'Angelo 34
Baia delle Zagare 37
Norman castle 36
Santuario di San Michele 35
Tomba di Rotari 35

O

opening hours 137
Ostuni 66
Cattedrale 68
Chiesa di San Francesco 66
Museo di Civiltà Preclassiche della Murgia Meridionale 67
Obelisco di Sant'Oronzo 66
Piazza della Libertà 66
Otranto 78
Baia dei Turchi 81
Basilica di San Pietro 80
Cappella dei Martiri 80
Castello Aragonese 79
Cattedrale dell'Annunziata 80

P

Padre Pio 39
Peschici 38
Al Vecchio Frantoio 38
Castello di Peschici 38
police 137
Polignano a Mare 57
Porto Badisco 79

public holidays 138
Puglia Imperiale 44

R

Rodi Garganico 39

S

sagne n'cannulate 72
San Domino 42
San Nicola 41
Santa Maria di Leuca 83
Basilica Santuario di Santa Maria de Finibus Terrae 83

T

tarantella 85
Taras (Taranto) 85
Cappellone di San Cataldo 87
Castello Aragonese 87
Cattedrale di San Cataldo 87
Chiesa di San Domenico 87
Convento Santa Chiara 87
Doric Columns 87
Museo Archeologico Nazionale (MArTA) 86
Palazzo di Città 87
telephone 138
The Great Apulian Aqueduct 81
time zones 139
tipping 139
toilets 139
tourist information 139
trabucchi 37
Trani 49

Castello Svevo 50
Cattedrale di San
    Nicola Pellegrino 50
Chiesa di Ognissanti 52
port 52
Scolagrande 52
Scolanova 52

Villa Comunale 53
transport 140
Troia 43
trulli 60

V
Valle d'Itria 59

Vieste 37
    castle 37
    cathedral 37
    Spiaggia di
        Pizzomunno 37
    Spiaggia di Scialmarino
        37

THE MINI ROUGH GUIDE TO
PUGLIA

Second Edition 2025

Editor: Libby Davies
Author: Solveig Steinhardt
Picture Editor: Piotr Kala
Picture Manager: Tom Smyth
Cartography Update: Katie Bennett
Layout: Grzegorz Madejak
Production Operations Manager: Katie Bennett
Publishing Technology Manager: Rebeka Davies
Head of Publishing: Sarah Clark
Photography Credits: All images Shutterstock except: Fondo Antiguo de la Biblioteca de la Universidad de Sevilla 24; iStock 8, 12CL, 12BR, 13TC, 13B, 14CL, 40, 44, 55, 56, 61, 65, 66, 73, 89; Leonardo 100; Public domain 23, 26, 28; © ARET Pugliapromozione/Andrea Ruggeri 103; © ARET Pugliapromozione/Helmut Berta 94; © ARET Pugliapromozione/Kash Gabriele Torsello 106; © ARET Pugliapromozione/Vanda Biffani 99
Cover Credits: Alberobello Shutterstock

About the author
Solveig Steinhardt is a travel writer, journalist and editor who lives between Tuscany, where she grew up, and Berlin. Her work has appeared in many travel outlets, including BBC Travel, *Michelin Guides* and the *Toronto Star*, and she is the former editor of travel magazines *Where Rome* and *Where Berlin*. Solveig loves to spend her time exploring the unbeaten paths of Southern Europe and is particularly passionate about the urban and natural histories of coastal areas, architectural details, lost dialects and local culinary traditions.

Distribution
UK, Ireland and Europe: Apa Publications (UK) Ltd; sales@roughguides.com
United States and Canada: Ingram Publisher Services; ips@ingramcontent.com
Australia and New Zealand: Booktopia; retailer@booktopia.com.au
Worldwide: Apa Publications (UK) Ltd; sales@roughguides.com

Special Sales, Content Licensing and CoPublishing
Rough Guides can be purchased in bulk quantities at discounted prices. We can create special editions, personalised jackets and corporate imprints tailored to your needs. sales@roughguides.com; http://roughguides.com

All Rights Reserved
© 2025 Apa Digital AG
License edition © Apa Publications Ltd UK

Printed in Czech Republic

This book was produced using **Typefi** automated publishing software.

No part of this book may be reproduced, stored in a retrieval system or transmitted in any form or means electronic, mechanical, photocopying, recording or otherwise, without prior written permission from Apa Publications.

Contact us
Every effort has been made to provide accurate information in this publication, but changes are inevitable. The publisher cannot be held responsible for any resulting loss, inconvenience or injury sustained by any traveller as a result of information or advice contained in the guide. We would appreciate it if readers would call our attention to any errors or outdated information, or if you feel we've left something out. Please send your comments with the subject line "Rough Guide Mini Puglia Update" to mail@uk.roughguides.com.